SMALL BUSINESS OWNERS SURVIVAL GUIDE

CRAIG THOMPSON

This book is dedicated to the great women in my life: Mom, My Grandma, My sister Suzie, My Daughter Holly and My Fiancée Bella.

Craig Thompson

ISBN Number: 145633395X
EAN-13: 9781456333959
Published in the United States by Amazon Books LLC.

"Fortune favors the bold."

Roman Poet Virgil (70 BC - 19 BC)

Congratulations on your momentous decision to start your own business. The dictionary definition of business is "a person, partnership or corporation engaged in commerce, manufacturing or the purchase of goods and services in an attempt to make a profit."

That may be the exact definition but it does not go far enough. Small business is the backbone of this country. According to Small Business Administration, small companies have produced over 65% of net new jobs for over the past 17 years in the U.S.

If you are not lucky enough to inherit wealth, two of the best ways to get it over the long term are to own your own business and the stock market. I am not an expert on the stock market... I am on starting and running a business. I hope this book helps you in your new business.

TABLE OF CONTENTS

Chapters	Title
1	Business Plan, Getting Funding
2	Setting Up Your Business
3	Company Name/Logo/Branding
4	Finding A Location
5	Marketing/ Advertising/ Public Relations
6	Putting Together A Team of Advisors
7	Setting Prices/Pay Rates
8	Signage And Merchandising
9	Vendors And Suppliers
10	Hiring Employees
11	Human Resources
12	Sales
13	Being Profitable/Cutting Expenses
14	Customer Service Training/Customer Complaints

TABLE OF CONTENTS

15   Know the Jargon/
         Business Dictionary
16   Hiring Top Managers/Management
17   Motivating Employees
18   Terminating Employees
19   Accounting and Sales Projection
20   Crisis/Risk Management
21   Setting Up Or Improving Your
         Website
22   Expansion/ M&A
23   Years 1, 5 & 10
24   Selling Your Company/ Turning It
         Over When You Retire
25   Conclusion

CHAPTER 1

CREATING A BUSINESS PLAN/GETTING FUNDING

On page 11, you will see an example of what should be included in a successful business plan. Think of a business plan as a road map for your business and everything that an investor bank or a credit union would need to know before taking a chance on loaning your business money.

The first thing that an investor or bank would want to know before they invest their money is whether you have a good business plan and whether you have a good chance to repay the debt.

In general, you must have an executive summary and a general company description. You need to describe what your company is going to do, whether it is in retail, manufacturing or services, what your main products and services are going to be, and other products and services.

They need to know your marketing plan, that you have a plan to market your products/services, how you are going to do public relations as well as advertise your products/services. Additionally, they need to know that you have an operation plan of how you are going to run the day to day operations of your business. This includes your management experience, they need to know that you either have management experience in the type of business you are opening or that you will hire professionals that are knowledgeable in the business.

They also would like to know that you have a team of professionals such as a certified public accountant (CPA), an attorney and additionally most credit unions or banks nowadays are going to require technical assistance or a consultant, something like I do on a flat fee or hourly basis. If you can't afford a professional consultant in the beginning there is SCORE, which is a free service through Small Business Administration and/or Micromentor.org, both organizations provide mentoring and business counseling for free by volunteer business executives. I will tell you more details about those organizations later in the book.

Another area that is required in the business plan is your personal financial statement. Normally, when you are an established business and you apply for a loan they pull out a report known as Dunn & Bradstreet, which is a credit report for businesses. Since your business is new you would not have any established credit yet, they are actually going to look at your own personal credit, including your spouse's if you are married, and they will look at your FICO scores.

FICO, which stands for the Fair Isaac Company, is a scoring system that the majority of banks and credit unions use to see your creditworthiness. The number score is between 400 and 800. It shows your debt to income ratio, your past history of paying your debt. The lower your score the higher the interest rate and if it is too low they will not loan to you at all.

Nowadays because the banks are so much stricter, they are also going to require that some of the startup money is your own money. Some banks are very strict that they require 40%-50% of the money to be put up into the business being your own money. There are special programs through Small Business Administration, where SBA guarantees 70-90% of the loan but you still need to have 10-30% of your own money into the business itself.

You definitely will need to have a business/financial plan, most banks require to you have collateral, either the title to your house, or to your car or to other property. This is because they want to know they have something of value to go after if you default. A lender also would want to see in this business plan 24-36 months of cash flow projections because they would like to see your ability to pay the loan back.

A business plan is very important and it is the first thing that you need to do when you are starting your business. After you have your business plan finalized, then you are ready to go for your financing or funding. The majority of people that start small business use their own money. They cash in a 401K, they cash in their savings, they either come up with the money themselves or if they don't have enough they usually go to their friends and family as their backing and startup money. This is a good way to go and you can do it two different ways.

Your friends or your family or investor group can invest and basically you will do a contract or promissory note to pay them back in a certain amount of time with a certain interest rate. It is always good to give yourself a few months of operation before you have to begin repayment, but let's say you borrow $20,000 at 10% interest and you have to start paying them back a certain amount per month until the loan is paid in full. They will probably want some type of collateral.

Another way is instead of being paid back is they will own a percentage of your business. This is the easier way but in the long run if your business is successful that is not as advantageous to you as it is to them. The other disadvantage is eventually when you want to expand or when you want to sell you have someone else that is involved in the equation, so you cannot just sell without buying back their shares or getting their agreement. Sometimes you may not have another choice but having a partner in your business is not always the best course to take.

When you are dealing with a bank or credit union it will be best to get referrals from your accountant (CPA), or attorney or someone that knows the banks that loan in your specific industry or your business. Credit unions are normally easier to work with and may have lower interest rates but not all of them do business banking so you may end up going to a regular commercial bank or consumer bank with a small business division.

Financing is a very big part of starting your company and the main thing to rem^{1}ember is that the bank is going to look at it from its own perspective and not from yours. So you have to convince the bank that you have a great idea. You have to convince the bank that you have great management; either yourself or your partner or someone that you hired that will be good at managing the company. You also have to show the bank that you are investing your own money into the company so you know how it looks from the bank's point of view. It wants assurance that it will get paid back.

So that is what you need to do, you need to put together a business plan and you need to either find friends and family that you can present this to.

———————————

However, just because they are friends and family you still need to be professional and present it to them and let them know what your 5 and 10 year goals are for the business.

SAMPLE BUSINESS PLAN

TABLE OF CONTENTS
Executive Summary
1. The Marketing Plan
1.1 Environmental analysis
1.2 Product(s)/service(s)
1.3 Customer demographics
1.4 Competition and competitive advantage
1.5 Price strategy
1.6 Advertising and promotional strategy
1.7 S.W.O.T. analysis
1.8 Market research
1.9 Market targets
2. The Operations Plan
2.1 Business structure
2.2 Scope of operation
2.3 Regulatory issues
2.4 Insurance
2.5 Business premises
2.6 Location
2.7 Production arrangements
2.8 Distribution (place) arrangements
2.9 Credit terms
2.10 Plant and equipment
2.11 Quality control
2.12 Memberships and affiliations
2.13 Communications
2.14 Trading hours
2.15 Commencement date

3. The Organization Plan
3.1 Organization structure
3.2 Skills required
3.3 Personnel
3.4 Resumes
4. The Financial Plan
4.1 Financial strategy
4.2 Establishment costs and source of funds
4.3 Balance Sheet projections
4.4 Profit and Loss projections
4.5 Expected Cash Flow projections
4.6 Break Even Cash Flow projections
Appendices
**Email for a free business plan template;
Craig@WorldwideConsultingLLC.com**

NOTES

NOTES

CHAPTER 2
SETTING UP YOUR BUSINESS

Here are some of the fundamental things that need to get done first.

1. You need to decide the legal status of your company.

Here are the most popular:

Sole Proprietorship: This is the quickest, cheapest and easiest way to set up your company. You are the sole proprietor/owner of your business. You may or may not need to file a fictitious name ad in your local newspaper depending on your local rules. While this may be quick, it has some downsides. You will have few legal protections. You and your personal assets may be liable personally if your business is involved in litigation or bankruptcy.

Partnership: This is similar to a sole proprietorship except it involves two owners or more. It is quick and easy. It also can leave you open to legal trouble. A partnership will include an oral/written partnership agreement but it is better written to clearly define the terms of the partnership. This will include many things but three very important items are:
1. Who does what in the business?
2. Is it divided equally or some other percentage ownership
3. What is the process if one of the partners

wants to sever their ties, what happens if one partner wants to sell or retire?

Consult an attorney to prepare your agreement.

5013c or Non profit: This works best for a charity or foundation.

Corporation: The advantages are 1) it is more prestigious than other business entities 2) In most cases it will give you some legal and tax protections. In most states, a corporation is an "artificial person." So technically, the corporation not you personally can be sued or declare bankruptcy without risking your personal assets. Many small businesses operate as a sub chapter S Corp. Consult a C.P.A. or Tax attorney to see if you qualify.

A corporation is more expensive to start. It also has more requirements such as having a board of directors, a quarterly/yearly meeting, more filing/taxes, and documents. You should have an attorney, CPA or Tax Attorney help you decide if this or another entity is best for you and your business.

LLC, Limited Liability Corporation: Similar to a corporation but most consider an LLC to have less requirements than a corporation.

P.A., Professional Association: Usually a law firm, C.P.A. or medical office is set up this way. There are other ways to set up a company but these are the most popular. If you do not have an attorney, you can set these up on www.Legalzoom.com.

2. Know the City/County/State and Federal Laws regarding your type of business.

Working from Home: You will not usually have zoning issues regarding operating/starting your business from your home unless you will be having customers/employees in and out causing parking or noise issues. Make sure to check with all of the following regarding your home office.

Your Condo or Homeowners Association
Your City and County Clerks Offices

3. Do a thorough check to see if anyone else is using the same business name. You may also be required to file a D/B/A or "Doing Business As."

4. Obtain City/County Business Licenses and Or Permits.

This is a requirement that does not cost much so don't skip it. It is called a City License or a Business License and in some places an occupational license. You will need to disclose your type of business, the address and number of employees.

5. Get your State and Federal Employer Identification Number (EIN).

For home based business you can use your social security number as your federal employer identification number but to present a more professional image, file Internal Revenue Service (IRS) Form SS-4 to get your Identification number. You also will then be able to buy wholesale and save sales taxes on some of your business purchases.

6. Most states require you to register your business. In some states, it is with the department of corporations.

In most states it is the office of the secretary of state. Here is a list of them:

List of Secretary of State Offices
Official Website Secretary of State of Alabama
http://www.sos.state.al.us/
Secretary of State of Arizona
http://www.azsos.gov/
Secretary of State of Arkansas
http://www.sos.arkansas.gov/
Secretary of State of California
http://www.sos.ca.gov/
Secretary of State of Colorado
http://www.sos.state.co.us/
Secretary of State of Connecticut
http://www.sots.ct.gov/
Secretary of State of Delaware
http://sos.delaware.gov/default.shtml
Secretary of State of Florida
http://oss.dos.state.fl.us
Secretary of State of Georgia
http://www.sos.state.ga.us/
Secretary of State of Idaho
http://www.sos.idaho.gov/
Secretary of State of Illinois
http://www.sos.state.il.us/
Secretary of State of Indiana
http://www.in.gov/sos/
Secretary of State of Iowa
http://www.sos.state.ia.us/
Secretary of State of Kansas
http://www.kssos.org/
Secretary of State of Kentucky http://sos.ky.gov/
Secretary of State of Louisiana
http://www.sec.state.la.us/

Secretary of State of Maine
http://www.maine.gov/sos/
Secretary of State of Maryland
http://www.sos.state.md.us/
Secretary of the Commonwealth of
Massachusetts http://www.sec.state.ma.us/
Secretary of State of Michigan
http://michigan.gov/sos/
Secretary of State of Minnesota
http://www.sos.state.mn.us/
Secretary of State of Mississippi
http://www.sos.state.ms.us/
Secretary of State of Missouri
http://www.sos.mo.gov/
Secretary of State of Montana http://sos.mt.gov/
Secretary of State of Nebraska
http://www.sos.state.ne.us/
Secretary of State of Nevada
http://sos.state.nv.us/
Secretary of State of New Hampshire
http://www.sos.nh.gov/
Secretary of State of New Jersey
http://www.state.nj.us/state/
Secretary of State of New Mexico
http://www.sos.state.nm.us/
Secretary of State of New York
http://www.dos.state.ny.us/
Secretary of State of North Carolina
http://www.secstate.state.nc.us/
Secretary of State of North Dakota
http://www.nd.gov/sos/
Secretary of State of Ohio
http://www.sos.state.oh.us/
Secretary of State of Oklahoma
http://www.sos.state.ok.us/

Secretary of State of Oregon
http://www.sos.state.or.us/
Secretary of the Commonwealth of Pennsylvania
http://www.dos.state.pa.us/
Secretary of State of Rhode Island
http://www.sec.state.ri.us/
Secretary of State of South Carolina
http://www.scsos.com/
Secretary of State of South Dakota
http://www.sdsos.gov/
Secretary of State of Tennessee
http://www.tennessee.gov/sos/index.htm
Secretary of State of Texas
http://www.sos.state.tx.us/
Secretary of State of Vermont
http://www.sec.state.vt.us/
Secretary of the Commonwealth of Virginia
http://www.commonwealth.virginia.gov/
Secretary of State of Washington
http://www.secstate.wa.gov/
Secretary of State of West Virginia
http://www.wvsos.com/
Secretary of State of Wisconsin
http://www.sos.state.wi.us/
Secretary of State of Wyoming
http://soswy.state.wy.us/

7. Know your local state and federal tax laws:

Having a C.P.A. or Tax Attorney is crucial knowing when you need to pay state sales taxes (usually monthly) and your federal estimated tax (usually quarterly). A recordkeeping or bookkeeping system will help with this. By far the most used is Quickbooks.

8. Print some business cards and brochures.

You need them as soon as possible. You want to keep your cash in the bank so don't go crazy. Here are the vendors/printers I use that are inexpensive but will give you the professional appearance you need: VistaPrint.Com and FedexOffice (Formerly known as Kinkos).

9. Lining up your Suppliers/Vendors.

This will be one of your most important decisions. Start with as many as possible and let them fight for your business. You may have to pay Cash On Delivery (C.O.D.) in the beginning. Eventually they will let you pay on 30-60 day terms. Always pay on time to ensure you get the supplies you need. You also should purchase from Staples, Sams Club, Costco, Craigslist.Org, and EBay. Some of them have special pricing for small businesses. On Craigslist and Ebay, you can also sell your products/services.

10. Getting Equipment/Office Furniture:

Many new companies lease their furniture, copier, etc. One reason is to conserve cash, another reason is you can get a professional look for a low price. The other reason is there may be tax benefits to leasing. The rule is to get the minimum you need. Yes you need computers but do they need to have 24 inch screen and surround sound if you own a shoe store? Probably not.

11. Choose a Bank/Open a Checking Account.

If you have banked for years with one branch and know the manager that should be your business bank. If not, pick one with multiple locations in case you want to expand. Compare prices and services.

12. Join a few networking or professional organizations.

Just because you are now self-employed does not mean you are on your own. Join Toastmasters, Rotary, Knights of Columbus or any others you may like. Not only is it a good way to get business, it may also help improve your business knowledge. If you are in a group for a few months and have not gotten any leads yet then find another group to join, you are not there for fun and games, you have a new business to run!

NOTES

CHAPTER 3
YOUR COMPANY NAME/LOGO AND BRANDING

"Words have meaning and Names have power."
---Plato

You will need a company name. Make it catchy, make it simple, think about the future. If you name your business Houston Shoes that is a fine name. What if you want to expand to Dallas? Or open a store in Florida? Now if Houston is your last name it may work but if you really want to keep your options open think big.... shoe town or shoe world are names that can work anywhere.

Your Company name needs to be memorable but needs to be easy to spell. Your company name should be positive and should convey trust and strength. A good example is Prudential and its Rock of Gibraltar logo.

Your Company name should explain clearly what your company does or sells. A very great example is Home Depot. The name should be short. Pick two or three names because one or two may not be available when you go to register your name with the state.

You will probably want to have some kind of logo. It does not have to be overly artistic, think of Ford, a blue oval with the company name in that famous font.

When doing a logo, remember it must be 100% original. Do not try to start with an existing logo and alter it. If you are artistic or know a graphic designer then you can design your own. Remember keep it simple. Do not use too many colors. Think clean and crisp. Do not have more than two fonts. It should relate to your business, it will have to print well and look good on a website. If you want to get a logo created at a low cost, www.vistaprint.com can help you.

After you have a great logo, go to www.legalzoom.com or to the United States Patent and trademark office website to register it : www.USPTO.gov

After that when you put your company name and logo on anything you can use the initials "TM" to show it as a registered trademark.

Branding is a word that has come into vogue in the last few years. But it has been around forever. U.S. Companies by far do a better job at branding than anywhere else. Branding is why Coke™, McDonalds™, and Levis™ are global icons.

You have to think about what your company makes or sells. Think about what you want your image to be.

Branding is how you will clearly deliver your company image. It will motivate your customers to buy on an emotional level. It will help you build customer loyalty and makes your company look credible. People buy from companies they like and make them feel comfortable.

NOTES

CHAPTER 4
FINDING A LOCATION

"In this place I take my stand. I can do no other. God help me. Amen." ----Martin Luther

In corporate speak this is called "site selection." You have heard the top three things that matter in real estate are location, location, location. It is very true. Years ago, I was once an executive for a small chain of mattress/furniture stores in southern California. After I came aboard we decided to expand. Most of the existing stores were Class B and C (Class A is the best locations and newest buildings, think the mall and the shiny skyscrapers downtown. Class B is next and Class C is usually in an older building in the not as good part of town.) Now those stores were profitable, let's say between 15-50,000 in sales per month. Let's say the average rent was under $2,000 per month.

My advice was to open across from the largest mall in the area. Now opening in the mall was an option but at over $20,000 a month in rent. No thanks. Plus you get mostly looky loos just walking around killing time until their movie starts. Now the rent across from the mall was still high at over $10,000 a month. It took a lot of convincing on my part but we finally did it. So what happened? The first month the store did over $90,000 in sales! We never looked back, once the owners saw the success. They could not deny the value of a great location.

So here are the things to help you get that great location. First get a realtor that does commercial real estate. Do not use your residential realtor. I was a realtor and an executive for a large real estate company. I know that an expert in residential homes is not what you need to find a commercial property. Your residential realtor could refer a good commercial agent to you. If you do not have a commercial agent you can find one on realtor.com and you can find space for lease or sale on loopnet.com

Here are the main things you and your agent need to consider when you are looking for your location.

Buy or Lease? For most there will not be a choice. Most new businesses do not have the funds to purchase. A lease can be for 5, 10 or more years, so you do not have to worry about having to move anytime soon. Your agent can provide or you can go online to the local library to get local demographics. You want to know the population centers where your most likely customers are.

Just because a location has a lot of traffic does not mean you will get a lot of customers. So look at the traffic patterns. But more important, look at accessibility: How easy is it to get in and out of the location? Is there adequate parking? Visibility? Is it easy to see? Will you be able to have good signage?

Traffic: How much is there? Is it the right kind of traffic? Is there public transportation within walking distance? Is there any competition close by?

I have never worked for the Fortune 500 companies but I do look to put my stores across the street from the Big Boys. Why? Because they spend millions to get people into their stores. I know customers compare 2 or 3 different stores before they buy. I will let the big store pay to get them there. They will see me and then it's over. I have better customer service, better salespeople and more flexibility on deliveries and I have lower prices.

Location costs: Make sure rent is not the only thing you consider. Is there extras you have to pay? Like parking, lawn care, maintenance. Here are the most common commercial leases:

Net Lease: You pay rent and a percentage of insurance, maintenance and operating expenses.

Triple net Lease: You pay rent and all operating and maintenance expenses.

Gross Lease: Tenant pays set amount while landlord handles all other costs.

Shopping Center Lease: Like a triple net but you may also pay a percentage of sales, you will have to be open certain hours. You have to follow strict rules about signage and deliveries. The landlord will usually reserve the right to relocate you.

Land Lease: You lease the land, you pay to build a building you pay all operating expenses, insurance and maintenance, all improvements, buildings, etc. revert back to the landlord when the lease is over. This is not a lease to get involved with unless it is the only land available and get a 10, 20 year or longer lease.

Consider factors like: does it have enough space for storage or extra stock? What is the crime rate in the area? Why is the spot available? Did the last business fail?

There are walk by stores like in a mall or in a busy downtown area. Here you will get a lot of looky loos just coming in with no intent to buy. But that's okay if you have great sales people you can make them buy if not now then in the future. The other type of location is called a destination store. If you are a stand alone without walk by traffic you will get a lot less traffic. For some businesses (car lots, furniture stores that is okay, when you do get a customer in you know they want what you are selling. So go sell them!

NOTES

CHAPTER 5
MARKETING ADVERTISING AND PUBLIC RELATIONS

Most people think marketing is sales. Actually marketing is not sales. Marketing, advertising, public relations and sales are four distinct different areas but they all have the same intent to get your name out there and to generate good public image but the bottom line is to generate sales. There is a position in a lot of companies, bigger companies, director of sales and marketing and vice president of sales and marketing. Marketing and sales are different areas but sales being so important it will have its own chapter later in the book.

We are now going to cover marketing, advertising and public relations. One good way to explain it is Target. Target as part of their marketing strategy decided that they are going to give a percentage back of all their sales to charity. That is a marketing strategy. When you see an article in the newspaper about Target giving back that is public relations. When you see an ad in the newspaper or you see a TV commercial about giving back this % that is advertising. When you go to the store and you buy a product because you feel good buying from Target because part of your money will go to charity that is Sales. That is the best way to explain all four parts.

One thing to keep in mind is you cannot just have only one or two ways to market, that is a recipe for disaster. You should have at least six or eight different areas that you get your customers from so where there is problem with one or two you still have customers from the other ways. Most of the way you are going to get your customers is simple, you are on a good location with good signage and you are going to have people that drive by and see you.

If you take my advice from earlier chapters and you put your store across from some of your big competitors, you are going to be able to use their millions of dollars in advertising that they spent to get customers in and then when they cross shop and find you and you have lower prices, better customer service and more knowledgeable sales staff then that is also part of your marketing.

Some of the other that you probably may or may not know about are going to be: TV, radio, direct mail. Those may or may not be affordable to you in the beginning but it is affordable for you to join Rotary, join Toastmasters, to have business cards with you in church, to join some community organizations, some charities to give out your business cards and brochures. Make sure everyone knows what kind of business you do and where your location is. Also get some fliers made up and pass them out wherever you are and if you don't have time to do it because you have to be working then hire a kid or have one of your kids or one of your nephews and nieces go out and pass fliers. Also depending on your city or county look to see if it is allowed you can also have a sign holder that can hold up a sign that talks about your business and they can also pass fliers at bus stops and in the corner to get people in.

Now, whenever anything happens in your business like you have your grand opening, you have a new location or you received some kind of award, anything like that then the best thing to do would be to send some kind of an article to that and fax it to your local newspapers and your local business journals. There are some websites such as prweb.com that helps you to get your name out on the web. Also there is the social networking that is really big now such as Facebook, Twitter. Make sure you have a page on each and if you don't know any about that your six year old kid or niece will be able to help you out with that.

There is also a very interesting new part of marketing and that is bloggers. You can get bloggers that will definitely send you business. I know of a new baby product and they got in with what was called mommy bloggers and that really helps jump start their business. Basically, in any kind of industry there is going to be blogs on there and if you can get them to be aware of you, your location and what you do then that will definitely generate business for you.

Now advertising is how you implement the marketing strategy that you have already decided. Part of your marketing is going to be trying to identify who your customers are, what age they are, what sex they are, what income level they are so that you can actually when you do your advertising try to hit your target market. This means you have to know the demographics of the radio or TV station or wherever you are advertising on so you try to get the most bang for your buck when you actually are advertising.

You should make a rule, most businesses do, set at least 1% to 3% of their sales aside for ongoing advertising. Direct mail, Sunday paper will probably be your most effective in most retail or sales type company situations in the beginning, they are going to be the most cost effective. Down the road you are going to look at cable TV, radio and regular television commercials. The best advice for this type of advertising is when you hire a radio station you are going to get a marketing professional with that or you can have or hire a marketing agency, the best thing to do is hire the best and then trust them to get your results.

Advertising and marketing are areas that you need to make sure that you have a professional image that is very concise on what your product is, what you do, why you do it better than others and why someone should come in.

A sale is always good but make sure that you do not have any kind of issues as far as bait and switch. If you are selling a product for $99 make sure that you have it if someone comes in. In a future article I will tell you how to make sure that your sales people are trained well enough so that they are not going to just sell that $99 that got someone in that they are going to try to upsell because they are going to make more commissions and everyone is going to be better off if they sell the $399 than the $99. But don't get yourself in trouble so make sure that you can back up everything that you claim in your sales and make sure that you have good sales people that are friendly and are waiting for when the person comes in.

Your marketing strategy should all be based around making your company looks professional and selling as much product as possible.

NOTES

CHAPTER 6
PUTTING TOGETHER A TEAM OF ADVISORS

"You are my advisor, you are always with me,
you preserve, protect and care for me." ---Atharva Veda

When you are starting your own business, hopefully you are an expert in what you are selling, making or your service but you may not have all the skills that are going to help you to be successful so you need to put a team together. A good team that you have checked their background or that were referred by their other clients, but the first three that you will need that should be the beginning of a long-term relationship will be your CPA, a certified public accountant.

The reason that you do not want a regular bookkeeper or accountant is that a CPA has extra training, extra requirements, also when a CPA signs off on your books it is usually good for the IRS or any other government agencies as being legitimate. So a CPA is definitely one of the first one you need to interview a few, find one that you are comfortable with and they are probably going to help you set up with a bookkeeping system either online or a written if you prefer and you don't like or trust your records to a computer. Quickbooks is by far the easiest and Excel also is one that is used by a lot of business owners. But you need to have a definite bookkeeping system and then you need to make sure to keep all of your records so that you can give to your accountant. And normally what you are going to do is what is called an estimated quarterly taxes, where you are going to pay your taxes for your business on a quarterly basis.

Another area to look into and definitely talk to your accountant is some businesses instead of worrying about payroll and company benefits and workman's comp and all that you need to do when you run a business is a thing called employee leasing. Basically you have an outside company that will take all of that for you, and basically you will just send them one check, keep track of the hours but basically the employees actually work for them and I will get to that in the Human Resources chapter. But definitely talk to your accountant to see if that is something that will be better for your company.

Your attorney is going to be the next adviser that you definitely should get as soon as possible. You can use Legalzoom and some other companies to just do your incorporation paperwork but you are going to need an attorney to do some of your paperwork and you should have an attorney to be there when you have things come up, contract matters, employees, or customer lawsuits, any kind of government agency issues with zoning or fines. A good attorney just like the accountant, try to get referrals from friends and family and people that are in business. Interview a few and make sure that you have a good relationship with an attorney.

The next advisor is a business coach or a business consultant. Now a lot of business owners do not think that this is worth the expense but a business coach or business consultant is definitely going to help you to bring the business acumen and experience that you may be lacking and they are also going to help you if you need help to interview sales people, to train.

If you can't afford a business consultant some consultants like myself included if I'm dealing with a client that has a new business, I will either work for a deferred payment where I will take less now and deferred it down the road or there are times where I also have done pro bono, where I have worked on a volunteer basis. I have also volunteered on micromentor.org, goodwill and we help businesses that are low income. There is also a very good program as part of Small Business Administration and is called SCORE and it is mostly retired, semi-retired business executives that volunteer to help most businesses right from business planning all the way through. If you can't afford a business coach or advisor then go to micromentor.org, or go to Small Business Administration and find the SCORE program. They will be able to help you, the only difference would be is that the consultant you hire is 100% working for you and it might be easier to actually get them on as needed basis. If you have questions and would like a referral of a good consultant in your area it could be me because I do travel.

Please email me at craig@worldwideconsultingllc.com.

NOTES

CHAPTER 7
SETTING PRICES AND FEE RATES

"Price is what you pay. Value is what you get."
---Warren Buffet

It may seem odd that setting prices and pay rate would be in the same chapter but in fact they go hand and hand. If you set your prices too low you cannot pay to get good talent, if you set your prices too high you are not going to get enough business and you are also not going to have enough profits for good pay rates.

Setting prices can be one of the tougher parts or can be a big challenge, you want to be competitive but you also want to be profitable. You want to make enough to pay your people well and also have enough to advertise and have enough put away for a downturn. There are different ways that you can come up with your price structure. One of the things you cannot do, however, is to get together with two or three other competitors and talk about pricing, this could be a big mistake and get you in what is called anti-trust. If you need advice on this, this is a good time to use your accountant, your CPA and also your business consultant or your business coach.

The easiest way to start thinking about pricing is to take all your expenses, your rent, your insurance costs, all your payroll costs, your inventory and start that way, so that your expenses and the costs of your goods are covered first then the profit can be added to that. You can also find online what the profit margins are for your industry. Some businesses like grocery stores have a very low margins. They have to sell a lot of products to make profit. While other businesses like retail, or some manufacturers the profit margin is so much higher because there is less competition and they also do less volume.

One of the rules in retail because sometimes the merchandise may sit on the shelf for a long time and you may have to sell it at a discounted price, is that you take your wholesale price and usually increase it by 50% or more. That extra 50% is not only going to give you certain amount of profit but it is also going to pay for your sales commission, your overhead like your rent and other expenses. Just make sure that you add up everything that you owe, all your expenses, whatever the cost of your item is and then put yourself in a 15% to 25% margin on top of that so you have a good profit margin to go by.

But this is not always realistic because you have to go a little bit deeper into your local market. One thing you can do is shop your competition. The larger national chains will change the pricing weekly so make a routine part of your week to shop two or three of your competitors and jot down the prices and make sure that you are competitive. If you are a little bit lower in price that is actually even better.

The key is not only to know all of your costs but also what your expenses are and take all that into account. You also have to know what your breakeven point, what is the minimum you can sell that without losing money. You also need to look at the economy, when the economy is in recession such as is now you need to be happy with a smaller margin but you can always increase pricing when the economy does better. The other side of that equation is that when the economy is like this, you actually do not have to offer as many raises because people are not going anywhere because there are not that many jobs. If people did leave you will have lots of applicants. Basically, you need to always keep in mind that there is always going to be someone that will be able to sell at rock bottom prices or even without the profit so you can't always have the lowest price but you can be among the lowest prices but you can make up for it with the smartest sales people and with more friendly salespeople, better customer service.

Now, let's look at your suppliers. You also have to shop around and make sure that you are getting the best price and best service when you are getting your supplies. If you are not you need to shop around and find a better supplier that is going to take care of you and get you better prices.

Pay rates: you may not have to worry about pay rates right away because it may just be you but eventually you will have employees. You cannot get away from paying the federal or state minimum wage where you are, you need to contact your local state employment department or labor board. You are also going to be required to hang up a federal and state minimum wage for your employees.

In most states minimum wage is pretty standard but that is going to be more for entry level positions. When you look at pay rates you need to look at a couple things, if you pay too much you are hurting your profits, if you don't pay enough you are not going to get very good people. So you need to kind of use a balancing act, what you can do is you can always go on monster.com and use their salary calculator and you can find out what the average pay is for that position in your area.

One thing that I always recommend is that the hourly wage should be lower than the total compensation package and I would always if it's a sales position I would want the majority of my person's money to be generated by selling product. If it's a management position, I would want maybe not the majority but maybe at least 25-30% of their compensation package to be from bonuses based on production and on performance.

If you do these types of compensation packages you will not have to worry about people that make their good hourly pay and they are not going to do extra to perform. You are not going to be able to watch them all the time. In fact once you have multiple locations you are going to have to trust the good people that are always trying to make more, if they are in a commission or performance based pay plan then you have a better chance to be successful at this. You still have to make sure even if it's a sales commission job that you pay minimum wage or even more but just as an example, instead of paying your sales personnel working in a car sales position or furniture sales job, instead of paying them $18/hr times 40 hours a week and hoping that they sell well, I will pay them $10/hr and 5%-7% percent or whatever it works out as to how you price your product but I will give them a percentage on each sale so that basically they can actually make more than the $18/hr that you originally thought of. They might be able to make $25/hr, but the extra on top of that $10/hr base is based on what they sell. So every week they are going to have incentive to sell more because they are not going to be happy with $10/hr, that is $20,000 a year on $10/hr, $400 a week, whereas if they make $25/hr, that is all of a sudden a $50,000 a year job.

So definitely your pay rate got to be competitive. If you don't have a good benefit package you are also at a disadvantage to bigger companies that's why you may want to look into employee leasing that offers all of the medical, dental or 401k that the large companies offer, which I will get into that in the HR chapter.

NOTES

CHAPTER 8
SIGNAGE AND MERCHANDISING

"Advertising moves people towards goods, merchandising moves goods towards people." ----Morris Hite

This chapter will be on merchandising but signage is also a very important part of your business. Now signage mostly involves the outside signs of your business and the most important part of the outside signs of your business is visibility. You went to trouble to get a very visible location where you need to have a visible sign so it is worth the extra a lighted sign so it can be on at night and in bad weather it can be seen from far away.

If you don't have money for an expensive neon or lighted sign in the beginning depending on your products you can look into what is called co-op advertising, that is where you see a pizza shop with the Pepsi or Coke logo on their sign. That was Coke or Pepsi paying for some or all of the sign to include their company logo on your sign. If you carry national products whether you are a furniture company, auto repair or restaurant, if you carry a national product you may look into co-op for your signage. Another thing to remember for your signage specially if you have neon or flashing lights is you have to check with your local county to see if it's allowable. The sign company is responsible for the permit but because you are the business owner you are the one that is ultimately responsible so it is better to be safe than sorry so look into all that.

You are also going to have interior signage and advertising material. The main thing is just to make sure that it is neat and crisp, don't overdo it, you still want to be able to see into your store for security issue, you want the police to be able to see in if there's a robbery so don't cover all your windows. Less is more so just keep it non-cluttered, make it look clean and make it look as professional as possible. All of the major office supply places from Staples to Officemax to FedEx/Kinko's all make banners and signs what is called POP, point of purchase materials.

The main purpose of this chapter is merchandising. Merchandising basically is a way to promote and it's also a way to display your merchandise in a way that is going to show it in the best light and also it's going to help you sell product. If you think about how a grocery store is set up that is merchandising 101 right there. Basically, they know that most people go in for milk, eggs, butter, bread so the convenient way would be for them to put those right where you walk in but no those are going to be all the way in the back so you have to walk by lots of other products so they have a lot of chance to sell you other products.

So that is also something that you can think of if you are advertising a $99 special to get people in the door that is not the first thing you display, you are going to put that all the way in the back so they have to walk by all your other merchandise to get to that product. If you notice in the aisles the prime spot is what is called eye level, so those are the more expensive, national brand products. In fact some of the manufacturers would even pay what is called shelf fee, they will pay the grocery store for better spots on the shelf except for in the kid's aisle then the aisle level is basically right where the kid is sitting in the cart, so they are very smart on how they place things so you need to pay attention to that also.

Make sure things are clean, things are not wrinkled, they look nice. The best example or one of the examples I would use is when I was an executive in a chain of mattress stores what we would do is the lower price beds we always sold as we didn't sell cheaper bed we sold less expensive good bed and we have the better, which is the middle price and then the best. But the lower priced or entry level beds that we kind consider for either a kid's room or for a guest room, we would show those in a twin size. So basically people will just see it in a twin size and it didn't really look as nice, the more expensive bed we would show in king size, where both husband and wife can get in it, we will have big fancy pillows and it looks just a lot nicer. We have no problem selling the lower priced item but it did not look as appealing and that is a psychological thing that you have to look at with merchandising.

Your more expensive product, the products with higher margins, those are the ones that you have to put in the best light and show in the best possible way. It doesn't mean that you can't money selling the lower priced item but you have to sell a lot more of them so of course if you make them a little bit less appealing you are not going to want to top down your product but you just want to use the good, better, best method which I will go more to in the sales chapter.

The fact is merchandising is something that you need to look at your competitors get ideas but the main thing is to keep things looking nice, have a plan in mind if you want to keep things in certain sections just you know think about when you go into Target, the men's section is all together, the women's is all together and shoes. You got to have things in certain areas but you also want to make sure you have plenty of aisle space. People do not want to be cluttered so try to have as much open space as possible and put small display items out and then put as much as you can in the storage so that you don't have a cluttered showroom.

The other thing to keep in mind with merchandising is that sometimes you are going to sell a national product that you will actually have to display it in a certain way if you want to carry that priced licensed product. The good thing about that is a lot of the trademark brands and licensing will also provide you with displays and with shelving and with different promotional materials that will help you to have a professional look and it will save you because you don't have to buy these things.

NOTES

CHAPTER 9
VENDORS/SUPPLIERS

Unless you are in a service business and even if you are you still need to get some supplies but if you are in manufacturing or sales business then this is even more relevant. Vendors and suppliers can be a partner that can give you quality products at good prices, deliver them when you need them and help you with your profit margins.

There is a new term in corporate America, it's called just in time warehousing, just in time merchandise. Basically that is when you don't need to have as much warehouse or storage space because you actually order things as you need them so that they basically come by FedEx or UPS right when you need them to put right out on the showroom floor. In a larger context it is having your deliveries but to your warehouse right at or right before the day that you go and bring it out to delivery so you don't always have a large stock on hand which saves you money. So basically you are ordering just when you need the items to go out to be delivered to customers. This is great as long as you have reliable vendors that are going to bring the product to you exactly when you need it.

That's why I recommend that when you first start out you use a few different vendors kinda let them fight out to see who is going to be the most reliable, gives you the best pricing. Most of the time vendors are going to be a little bit leery on giving you credit or terms when you first start buying from them so in the beginning you probably have to pay cash on delivery and give them a check right when they deliver your supplies. But after a certain amount of time they should be giving you terms because that will actually help your cash flow. If you can actually get your stock delivered and not have to pay it for 30 or 60 days on terms by that time you should have recouped your money from your customers. So basically you are not going into your savings or into your account you are actually using customer's money to buy your supplies and then there is profit on top of that if you have your merchandise priced properly.

Once you get a little bit bigger and you have employees you need to make sure that in your employee manual that you have a policy against employees getting any kind of extras or any kind of kickbacks from suppliers. This will happen quite often where supplier will offer usually an upper level management employee some extra kickbacks to throw business their way. This is not what you want to have happening in your company, it is a way that your business can lose money because that supplier may not have the best product, might not give you the best terms, and might not give you the best prices. Make this very clear in your employee manual that any type of anything or any gifts or anything that can be considered a gift or inducement is going to be grounds for immediate termination.

There are times if it's disclosed and above board and if you approve it. We have had suppliers that will actually bring all our company and pay for our dinner or bring us to a trip or something like that, that I don't mind as long as you are aware of it. As long as that is something they are doing as a thank you for your business. That is okay because you are smart enough to know when you have a good supplier. A good supplier and a good vendor is like a partnership and basically they succeed when you succeed so if you have a really good supplier and they want to thank you for your business that is okay.

What I don't want to have you allow is an employee enriching themselves without your knowledge to throw business to a certain company, that should not be allowed. But if you have a good supplier make sure you pay them on time, make sure that you send them other business and you can have a long and successful relationship that will help both of you succeed.

NOTES

CHAPTER 10
HIRING EMPLOYEES

"Surround yourself with the best people you can find, delegate authority, and don't interfere as long as the policy you decided upon is being carried out."
-----Ronald Reagan

There will be nothing since you decided to open your business and what your products or service will be that will be as important as hiring employees. One of the most important positions to hire will be sales people and sales managers. I'm going to give a few tips from one of my previous books called 101 Tips to hiring top sales people and sales managers. I will give a few tips in here but if you want to go more into it, you have to go to Amazon.com and order the book or you can email me at craig@worldwideconsultingllc.com and I will give you that information on how to order that book.

The best way to hire someone is to get someone that is a referral from a friend or family or a business acquaintance, somebody in one of your Rotary clubs. If you get someone that is referred you know their background. That would be my first option, after that there are a lot of ways, low cost ways to recruit people. The Small Business Administration has a free website where you can post jobs for very qualified people. They like hiring veterans, they are natural leaders they are also disciplined and they know how to get the job done and they think quick on their feet.

There are also other programs through your state's unemployment department or labor board that can help you to hire people without the expensive ads. But it's also worth it to spend a few hundred dollars to run an ad on monster.com and also on Sunday papers you can advertise for applicants. Just keep it simple, just simply put the position any previous experience that you want and an email will make it a little bit easier because you can weed through a if you get a lot of emails then you can just weed through those that are non qualified. But if you want someone right away then putting your phone number will be the quickest. You will get a lot of headhunters and salespeople but that is just part of it.

But basically just run a very simple ad, the less words you put in the cheaper it will be for you. You need to start thinking about when you actually do your interviews. I will put some sample interview questionnaires and some other things that will help you prepare when you do these interviews. But I'll throw out some things that you have to look out for as far as legal matters.

If there is a physical requirement, legally you can ask, if the person is going to occasionally load/unload things that are 50lbs or more that can be a physical requirement so that you can legitimately get away as part of the job. Let's say your business is open on Sunday, you can't come out and ask someone "do you go to church on Sunday?" That is not legal, whether someone goes to church or not is their personal business and they don't need to disclose that to you and you can't use whether they go to church or not as a reason not to hire them.

But if working on Saturday or Sunday is a requirement of the job then all you have to do is state that. This job requires that you work on Saturdays or this job requires that you work on Sundays or nights. Is that a problem for you? Then you leave it to them to decide whether they can or cannot meet the requirements of the job. Same thing if the job requires that they drive occasionally to a post office, to a bank or to another location. If you have an opening somewhere else, someone having a car is not an issue in some jobs where they can take the train or the bus or walk to work. But if it's a requirement in the job then you can ask it.

Here is where you have to make sure that you don't get in trouble. If you require something from one employee that this employee has to have a car or this employee has to be able to lift this minimum weight, you can't choose after that. If that's a requirement of the job it's got to be a requirement for everyone in the job from then on. You can't discriminate based on sex, you cannot discriminate based on race, you cannot discriminate based on any of those factors. What you do is you need to find the person that is best qualified, the person that has the best personality and the person that you think will fit in with your company and your culture. You do get to choose who you hire but be very careful as far as giving everyone the same courtesies. Everyone is allowed to apply.

How long your interview is will depend on you. Anybody that you start interviewing within 10-15 minutes you have a good chance and the longer someone stayed with you of course the more interested you are by your asking questions. That is another important part of the interview process is asking questions. If you are talking all the time you are definitely doing it wrong. You need to do either one to ask some questions and let them talk. The more they talk the more you will get insight into their personality.

If someone is very defensive, if they are not very friendly or very expressive I would not hire them. You do not want to have someone with customer service issues that is not friendly. You can pretty much tell someone who is just looking to get a paycheck and they are not really interested in doing well or advancement or any of that. If you have a good applicant in front of you, they are going to be very friendly, they are going to be able to tell you what they can do for your company. They will also ask questions about advancements, and the pay rates, bonuses and all those kind of things. If all they're asking you about is when you're off, vacation time and things like that just go with your gut. A good employee is going to stand out against all other applicants.

Usually a good rule is if you have one opening you probably have to talk to about 25-30 people on the phone and will probably at least interview 10-15 people in person. What I always recommend is you narrow those 10-15 down to 2 or 3 and then you have a two interview process, the first interview being a quick 15-30 minutes or longer if they are good. Basically the first one is to get to know them, see that they came dressed appropriately for an interview, and that they are on time. Then you set up the second interview, because by the second interview maybe you found someone that you like even better, the second time they could be late which is usually a big no and a big red flag not to hire them. If they can't be on time for their interview, if they cannot dressed right for their interview and if they are not prepared then how are they going...

At the interview that is the best impression they are going to make on you. Everything after that is usually downhill. The interview better be the best that you can see. If you narrow it down to 2 or 3 you usually will have somebody that will stand out and you will definitely know that you made the right choice.

Basically, you have to look at them also interviewing you because the best people are usually going to have more options. If somebody is desperate and they will take anything then they are probably desperate for a reason. The very best people, the smartest, the best personalities they have more than one options so you also have to be on your game.

It means you also have to dress professional, if you own a company then you should dress like you own a company. If you work in a warehouse or a service job that doesn't mean you can't have a pressed shirt and clean. If you are interviewing on that day, dress it up a little bit more, make sure your office is clean and organized. Make sure that you have time set aside when they come. If you are on the phone and it seems that you do not really care who is in front of you then they are going to really take it seriously that you are interested and they are just going to find another job.

Having top employees are going to be the best way that you are going to be successful because you are not going to be able to do everything. You have to hire people that are better at you, smarter than you in certain areas and you just have to manage them and let them do their job and it will be great. During the interview I always look for eye contact, big smile, just a really good personality. Even if it's not for a sales position you still want to have good customer service whether it's a receptionist, a sales person, an office worker and even delivery person that delivers to customers. Everybody has to have good customer service skills. If someone has a poor attitude and just doesn't want to be there and just looking for a paycheck then let them work for your competition and run them into the ground. You want good people and that's what you should expect. There is a saying that if you expect the best sometimes you'll get it. So, when you're hiring people expect the best and you may get it.

Once it comes down to the final interview and I narrowed it down, I do like to find out what other positions they are interviewing for, what their former and what their expected pay rate is. Like I told you in an earlier chapter I like to take a compensation package and break it up so basically a percentage of the compensation is based on bonus and based on commission. If you have someone who is nervous about that and does not like that plan then I would move to the next applicant. If someone is confident in their sales skills and their management skills they are not going to have a problem with that package, in fact they would like it because if you lay it out to them the right way they will see that they can make more money if they are top producers. So find out what they are looking for, it is always good to find out whether they need to give a two-week notice at the job they are now at. That's not a bad thing I mean sometimes it's a pain if you need someone right away but if they are willing to give a two-week notice and they are professional that means they will treat you as a professional if they ever leave your company and at least they will give you proper notice and enough time for you to hire someone new.

Find out all these details, find out if they have vacations or any time off that they set up any time soon. You have to let them know about your benefit package, if you don't have one yet then let them know that you will be getting one soon because if you don't have benefits it will be tough for you to get good people. But there is also the employee leasing that I have mentioned before and I will go more into details in the Human Resources chapter.

Basically, you lay out why this company is good, if you have a new company some of your prospective applicants may be worried about whether you are going to go out of business. But if you let them know that they are getting in on the ground floor opportunity that the future expansion, future managers, district managers, vice presidents are going to come from the people that start with you now. That will be something that will be really interesting to a lot of top quality applicants. Also let them know about your background, let them know that even though you just started your business you actually have been in this industry for how many years and your education just so that they can have more confidence that this is not going to get out of business soon and that they are not taking much of a risk by coming with you and that is a good thing.

Once you decided to hire someone, the first thing you want to do is make sure that they have all of the legal paperwork. There are some government websites, the IRS and the immigration department that has great websites and the links are IRS.gov and the homelandsecurity.gov. Basically, you can actually send in copies of their paper work to make sure that they are legitimate. But you need to make sure that you have picture id, which State driver's license or state id would count and passport would also count, you also need to have social security card, if they are not citizen then you need to have copy of their green card, which is their permission to work in the country and you also need a copy of their auto insurance if they are going to be driving. If they don't have any of these then do not hire them until they have them and also verify the documents. There is also an e-verify that you can use online.

Basically, it's on you and you don't want to risk your business, you don't want to risk a fine, you don't want to risk anything by hiring someone that is not in the country legally. Make sure to do everything legitimately, don't try to hire someone off the books, don't try to hire someone that has fake papers or is missing some documentations, it's not worth it.

As far as pay scales we've talked about that earlier but if you have someone in front of you that is very qualified and is asking for a little bit more pay than what you planned or what you budgeted for. There are two different ways to handle it, one if they are really good you can do it. Another that I try do is I try to meet them halfway and I say "look this is the pay for starting but if you do well after 90 days I'll look at it and then after your one year we also do evaluate your payroll and do your evaluation each year and if you deserve a raise then we can look at it then but you can always get this by increased performance or increased sales."

One other thing when hiring new employees is it will save you a lot of time and a lot of trouble to make sure that when you are screening the employees, when you narrow it down from the 10 that you have seen down to the final two and then take the final two to the one that you actually want to hire is that you do a full background check. I will give you some links, one is called Source.com, that does background check you can do everything by fax and it is very inexpensive. In some positions if it's a truck driver or something sensitive, a drug test could be in the works. Make sure to check their employment and educational history to make sure that it is all legitimate. The other thing I would recommend and I will put a blank template but make sure that your person is willing if it's a sensitive position to sign a confidentiality agreement, which means that things that he learns, different marketing techniques, and different products that you have coming out, that they know that if they disclose that or leak it to another company that they are all to stay trade secrets of your business.

NOTES

CHAPTER 11
HUMAN RESOURCES

"You don't win the Kentucky Derby with a slow donkey and a whip, you win with a thoroughbred.......and if you are lucky enough to have a thoroughbred let them run."

------Author unknown

The most important part of your business is going to be your people. Human Resources is about taking care of your people but making sure that you take care of yourself and you look out for your company. Unfortunately, because our society has become very litigious and employees specially disgruntled employees will sue the company. Part of smart Human Resources will also be thinking about protecting the company when you are dealing with employees, when you are dealing with customers and when you are dealing with vendors.

You need an employee handbook. If you email me I can send you some sample templates. This is something that you would want to get together with your business coach or business consultant and also have it look over by your attorney to make sure it is legal in your area. But you want to have an employee handbook, it can just be a small one and you can add to it but you want to have policies and procedures that your employees read when they first come to your company, they sign saying that they understand it and if they violate that you need to have documentation.

The most important thing in all human resources and all employee issues specially discipline is documentation. Even if you verbally give a warning to someone about being late, about whatever it is you start to document it because six months to a year from now you will not remember that. If they do the same thing again then you need to do a written counseling statement or what is called a write up. Here is a sample of a blank one that you can customize to your company.

The fact is that once an employee works for your company in different states they are going to have different rights. Some states are at will, some states do not even have a reason to fire them, other states the employees have a little more rights so it is better if you have documentation. The bottom line is that you don't want to fire good employees unless you attempted to correct their behavior and they won't respond and basically you need to get someone better. There is an expression that "if you can't change your people change your people." General Electric has a practice for many years where the bottom 10% where they always do a performance review and the bottom 10% each year was always let go, the theory was that you are only strong as your weakest link and if you are constantly weeding out the weakest in the bottom then that your chain or your workforce will always be stronger.

Dealing with problem employees is not easy but if you have a policy manual that they understand, if you are consistent, if one person is late and you let them get away with it and then another person is late and they don't get away with it then that can create animosity in the workforce. But the fact is top performers do sometimes get special treatment. But instead of letting a top performer be late I will just alter their schedule, if they can't get in to work at 8:30 in the morning it's okay

I will just have someone else to open up and that's all I care about. I will let them come in at 9:00 or 9:30 or would save on hours and they are not late and they got there on their scheduled time.

Special schedule is something that you are allowed to do. But if someone is supposed to be at work at 9:00 they need to be there at 9:00. Preferential treatment is something that is a little bit of a gray area but it is just a fact that top performers that if you don't treat them well they can go somewhere else. You don't want to have a bunch of mediocre or average or below average employees.

Remember Jimmy Johnson once used or gave the story about his super bowl champion Jimmy Johnson talking about he was considered a very tough coach but he had three hall of fame players that helped him win super bowl. Those players were Enith Smith, Troy Aikman and Michael Irving, and he was tough everyone and he was tough on them but they also got a little bit of preferential treatment because they were the starts and they were the ones that made everything happened. One time a reporter asked when he was asked what would happen if he catches one of the regular players sleeping and he said that he would yell in their ear or he would fire them. As for one of the triplets if they fall asleep in one of the team meetings and he said he'd turn off the lights and give them the blanket. Just maybe a bit of an exaggeration but basically if you have good people you need to take care of them.

Now one of the ways that employees stay happy is you need to put them in their best position. If you have someone that is very good at sales put them in the office doing accounts payable or accounts receivable is not a good option. If you have someone that is better at paperwork they should be the one in the office, if you have someone that is better at customer service they should be the one in charge of that. Cross training is also very important, this is something that the military does but if you have a receptionist that is out sick and no one else knows how to do the job how are you going to do business that way that is not smart.

If you have at least two or three other people that know how to do all the other different jobs, so when the receptionist is out you can have someone from the office, someone from sales, you can have someone else they will not do the job as good as the receptionist but at least it will get done that day. Basically don't let anybody become such a specialist that no one else knows how to do their job. For one, they will try to use it and hold you hostage and try to get raises with it, for two people are not always at work, people get sick, people have family emergencies, people have funerals that they have to go to, people quit jobs all of a sudden without notice so you shall always be prepared so cross training is something very important.

Now you are going to have to do training of your employees and I will get to that in the next chapter but one part of training that is under human resources part is sexual harassment training. Your employee has to understand that sexual harassment cannot be allowed with employees, with customers, with vendors at all. They have to understand that an area now that is very important and you don't want to get fined, you don't want to get sued and you don't want to open yourself up to litigation because of that. There is a website that I want to tell you about that is very good and they do have some sexual harassment, diversity training, business ethics, they have a lot of different training and they can be provided online and you can just set your people in and put on a computer screen or order a DVD and watch it. The website is www.hrclassroom.com, it's a good site, it has a lot of good things that can help you.

One area that we have to go into once we start talking about employee that is having issues whether it be they've made a sexual harassment claim, whether they have been written up plenty of times and you've put them on some probationary period where if they get another write up for the next 90 days you have to terminate them. You need to remember that you have to keep everything based on their performance. Don't get personal with it, don't look at it as personal but just make it all about business, only point out the business related things that they are doing wrong. Keep it to the facts : On September 15, of this year this employee was 30 minutes late without calling, this is a second occurrence if this occurs again there will be a termination. If you do that and you get your employee to sign that and if they won't sign it you write on "refuse to sign" and put that you made them aware of it. They don't need to sign but if they will not sign that's pretty much shows that they don't respect you as their supervisor and you probably should start looking for a new replacement.

But the bottom line with human resources is document, make sure that they are trained and if after you give them the training have them sign that they received it. Have a good employee file with all of these so that if you have to go to with the unemployment board or if there is a lawsuit you have documentation. I've been before many unemployment boards, one that I went to in particular we were being sued by a former employee who we had fired for incompetence and when he was being fired there was $1200 missing from his drawer, it just so happened that instead of firing him that day I suspended him without pay but I actually wrote him up and in the counseling statement I put in there that he was the one responsible for the money in his drawer, that he was the only one with the key to his drawer and I also made him to sign a promissory note promising to pay back the money if we could not find it before he came back from suspension. During the time of suspension we looked into everything and he tried to blame another coworker, we could not find any kind of proof that the other co worker stole the money so he ended up terminated. He tried to sue us, we gave him his final check, it came down where the judge did not even listen to his side very much because she said why would you sign this paper and if you are the only one with the drawer who else is responsible for the money. I told the judge that basically he either took the money or he did not secure the money so either way he is negligent and he deserved to get fired.

So never accuse someone if you don't have proof of it but if you have policies and procedures set up the right way and if you document things if you get before a court, a judge or labor board you are going to win every time because of documentation. Don't worry about being their friends, don't worry about being popular, let them be the ones to hang themselves. You want to keep good employees and get rid of the bad ones but you want to do it the right way so it doesn't cost you money. I always have a saying where "I wanted my employees very very happy or very very nervous." The meaning of that is if they are good employees I want them to love to come to work and I want them to enjoy their job and I want them to stay with me for a long time but I also don't want people to wonder what their status is. Basically if they are bad employee they always knew that they have to straighten up or they're going to be gone. That's why if they are good employees I want them to be happy but if they are bad employees I want them very nervous because they knew if they don't straighten up they are gone.

NOTES

CHAPTER 12
SALES

"The sole purpose of marketing is to sell more to more people more often at higher prices. There is no other reason to do it."
-----Sergio Simon

Sales is one of the most crucial parts of your business. Even if you are no matter what business you are in sales is a part of it, whether you sell online, whether you sell business to business, whether you sell retail. Sales, even if you are a service business, a repair business if you don't have customers, if you don't sell something and if you don't sell at a profit you won't be in business long.

There is a pretty simple sales process and I do have books more about Sales and Closing and all that and if you want to order books that are more detailed and go into a little more depth then just go on our website www.worldwideconsultingllc.com and you can purchase them on there.

But the first part of selling is having a good salesperson that is very friendly and knowledgeable. The first thing they will have to do is prospecting. There will be some customers that your advertising and your marketing will get into the door but for a lot of you that sell outside sales and also for any other type of sales you want to have salespeople that are able to prospect on their own. Part of the prospecting is called their "personal sphere of influence."

Everyone of your salespeople will have friends and family that are in their lives or you should have salespeople that are involved in different organizations like Rotary, Toastmasters, Knights of Columbus and The Elks. Basically the more people that they know the bigger sphere their influence is and this is also a way to get prospects and get customers. Prospecting is one of the first parts to the sales.

The next part is the first contact. On the first contact when a salesperson is first meeting someone the first thing they need to do is they need to work on building a rapport and getting to know the person. If you are the stereotypical salesperson with the loud checkered suits, and a bunch of gold and just a loud mouth that talks a lot and doesn't listen the person is going to be on defensive and they're going to think you're just another typical salesman that wants their money and they're just going to clam up. If you hire people that are friendly and just good people and they generally genuinely want to know about people and they want to hear about their jobs and want to hear about their families then that person will allow your customer to let their guard down and they will actually have a better chance of selling them.

The thing that is important about sales is you need to learn how to let the person buy your product instead of trying to sell it to them. If you force something on someone they're just going to cancel it, or they're not going to be happy. If you let someone buy it they are going to be happy with what they have and they're going to tell their friends and family and then you will have more business referrals. Basically your initial contact is when you just want to be friendly and you just want to start asking questions.

The art of selling is to solve the person's problem, they came in with a problem. They have a sore back so they come into the mattress store to buy a better mattress. Their car is starting to have problems and their car is old and they come into your car lot because they want a new car. They come in because they have a problem your job is to figure out how your product can solve their problem. It's all about features and benefits. If you tell them how your product is going to help solve their problem, if you're nice to them, if you believe in your product you are going to make a sell.

One thing you do have to make sure, if you are selling a house, selling a car, selling shoes you want to know who the product is for. Unless it's a father and mother coming in buying a bed for their kid's room or a car for their teenager as a surprise you are going to want to have a the person that the product is for or you're going to want to talk to the decision maker. You don't want to go through a whole presentation and then at the end say "well, I'm just looking out for my friend, looking out for my boss but I will have them get back to you." Why waste your time? You find out who it is for. If someone sends their assistant in to get information about their product, give them a brochure, give them your card and try to set something up with the decision maker. Sometime the assistant maybe in a position to actually purchase for their boss, make sure to ask all those questions. But in the beginning of the presentation you just want it to be non-confrontational and start asking questions.

Then you go into your sales presentation. In some businesses the presentation can be 5 minutes. If you're selling shoes there's not a whole lot that you got to explain that is going to take you a long time, if you're selling a car that may take longer, if you're selling a house that definitely takes a lot longer, if you're selling insurance. I'm not going word for word of what you'd say because every product is different. But this is something that if you were a top salesperson in your industry before you are going to know basically how to put together a sales presentation. Sometimes you might want to use a sales book and a lot of people do that because people learn in a lot of different ways and some people are more visual. So instead of talking to them if you have something visual it also can actually stimulate another one of their senses and that will actually help. But if you are not sure of how to put together a sales presentation for your product that would something that you want to get your business coach or trainer to help you with.

But the main thing about a sales presentation is it needs to sound very conversational, it shouldn't sound like a canned speech. But you want to make sure that you hear it a few times from your sales person so that you know that they are covering all the important facts. But you do want to get into why your product is better and you want to ask questions about what they're looking for and then you want to demonstrate and make sure that you're definitely getting to the root of what their problem is. Give them the features and benefits of why your product is best.

The next thing they're going to do is they're going to give you objections. Objection is a good thing. If you overcome the objection that means you get to make a sale. So when you get objection don't look at that as a bad thing. Now handling objections is something that will be a challenge when you're new but as it goes on you'll actually look whatever the objection is acknowledge it, repeat it back to the customer so that you know that you got it right. But an objection, all that is they're just asking you for more information.

If you give them enough information they're going to buy from you so an objection is not a bad thing but one thing, one little trick you can do when someone is continuing to bring up objections what I want you to do is Okay, whatever their problem is I want you to pretend that you can overcome that. Like if they say I would buy it if it's $599 then you're going to do it. Get their confirmation that they're going to do it because they might just be wasting your time. But if they actually come back and say yes you can then say I don't have the authority to do that but let me get someone on the phone, let me call my boss and if we can do it then I'm going to do whatever I can to try to get this for you.

Now the most important once you passed the presentation and the objections is to ask for their business. Never be shy to ask for the business and to go for the sales. Here are some signals that someone is asking about buying. If you're selling someone a house and they start talking about whether my bed would fit in here, whether if my china cabinet would fit on that wall, they're already picturing themselves in the house, that's a buying signal. That is something that you can use to start closing. You can use a very simple close like you know this is really a great house if you are interested we really need to go back and put an offer in today so you don't lose it. That is a close, it's a simple close, it's not a hard close. You probably should think as you need to ask for the sale 7 to 10 times every time you're in a presentation. Some sales people just do a presentation they hope the person buys. That's not what you want. You want a closer.

If someone asks you about colors, about availability, if they ask you about warranty, if they ask you about other things questions about your business how long you have been in business. If they start asking about service plan and they want a sample, those are all things that you need to look at as buying signals. So quit talking you're done with your presentation when they start asking buying questions, when they start asking things like that you need to quit talking ask for the sales and give them the opportunity to say yes. Give them the alternative close, would you like this delivered on Tuesday or Thursday? Would you like this car in silver or grey? Those are alternative close. Offer them incentive, if I can get you this 10% discount because you're a first time buyer, would that get you to do it today? Lead them through a series of little yeses and then you'll get to do the big yes. Don't give up too soon because if they're still there and they are enjoying it then you still have a chance.

Never lie to a customer, always be direct with them. Be knowledgeable about your product, be professional at all times. First you are going to do the paperwork after you do the sales, let's assume you did the sales. There's also a part of sales that is important that a lot of salespeople do not really do as good a job on and that is follow up. You need to have a rolodex or a computer log with all your customer information so you can keep up and do birthday cards. But the first thing you need to do when you make the sale is send them a thank you card. Be professional, don't make it personal, just thank them for their business and put some cards in there and let them know that you'd appreciate any referrals. Because basically what you can look forward to as a professional salesperson is that every year that you have business and you have all these people with your referrals out there, and cards out there that you should be able to increase your business and increase your sales exponentially each year if you have a good system of a follow up.

Also don't be typical, don't lie, don't bad mouth the competition, don't gossip, don't say things about other companies' clients. Just be a professional, be friendly but don't be overfriendly, believe in your product, make sure that you are dressed professionally and you will do very well with sales.

NOTES

CHAPTER 13
INCREASING PROFITS/CUTTING EXPENSES

"If you mean to profit, learn to please."
----Winston Churchill

Without making profit your company cannot survive. Everything you do, everything you buy, everyone you hire should have a positive impact on profit. If they do not then maybe you do not need it or them.

One way to increase profit is to increase traffic into your location. You have to know how many people come into your store/office. So over a 7-10 day period, count how many people come in. With that number (let's say 100 people) you next need to add up the number of sales and the total dollar volume. Let's say you made 8 sales with a total sales volume of $6,000.00 from these numbers you have an 8% closing ratio and your average sale is $750. Based on this data you can increase sales two or three ways.

1. Increase the total number of people. If you continue your 8% closing percentage, if you bring in just 3 people per day this will increase sales over 10%.

2. Increase your closing %. If you have better trained salespeople, you can increase sales without getting more people in the door. In fact, should you just increase the closing percentage to 12% that would be an extra $30,000 a year in sales.

3. Increase your per sale average. If instead of having an average sale of $750 each increasing this to

$850 would increase yearly sales by $28,800 without bringing in any additional customers!

Adjust your pricing. Your prices may be high and you may be losing business to a lower priced competitor. Or your prices may be too low and you have made it impossible to make a profit at this price level. The answer? Shop your competition weekly so you can keep your pricing competitive.

Increase your product line. Another way to increase profits is to offer more products. Pick products that compliment your existing product base but have little or no start up costs. Here are some examples:

If you have a restaurant that is open for lunch and dinner, consider opening for breakfast or offering delivery.

If you own a car dealership you can offer an extended warranty insurance or an oil change/maintenance plan each sale.

If you own a furniture store, offer to Scotchgard/fabric protector on each item sold.

Have links to related products on your website and you can get commission for it:

Example: You are a real estate company on your company website. You have links to your preferred mortgage company, home inspector, etc. If legal in your state you can have links to their websites and earn a commission each time they get a new customer from you.

Set sales goals and make sure your people meet them. In different industries with many different employees I have always done the best in the companies I have worked for. What is my secret?

It is mainly because I am great at recruiting and hiring good people. If you know you can hire someone great you will not tolerate sales people that are not pulling their weight. Have clear and obtainable sales goals. Give your people the training and the tools to get them. If they do not then hire someone better. The biggest key to increasing profit is: having great people, keeping them happy but making sure they continue to perform.

Cutting Expenses

There are ways you can cut costs and the money saved will go right to the bottom line. Make sure there is never over time unless there is an emergency. Overtime is usually time and a half. It is a waste of money. Hire a temp, a part timer or move people around to avoid it.

Make sure you are in charge of the thermostat and have preset vendors. Do not plan any purchases over a certain amount ($500 or more for example) without your signature.

Look into allowing employees to telecommute from home if your business is computer or phone based.

Move files and storage to an offsite location, this will make a room for desks/employees.

Instead of travel use conference calls when possible.

Join a barter or exchange club. If you trade items it is cheaper than buying them.

Interns. Contact your local community college to get free help. They get real world experience.

Cut all advertising/marketing that you cannot prove is making you money. If you cannot say it is paying for itself cut it.

Buy used furniture equipment, etc.

Buy on Craigslist and Ebay.

Be creative. I remember when I first started at Prudential Real Estate. I was looking over the books and I saw they spent over $5,000 a year on catering. This was mainly holiday parties and the monthly/weekly meetings with over 50 realtors. I cut that catering budget to just a few hundred dollars. How? Every meeting we had dozens of vendors begging to come to talk to my agents, home builders, mortgage companies, termite inspectors, title companies. So this is what I did if a company wanted to talk to my people. First I checked them out to see if they had good references, insurance, etc. If they checked out then I told them they could talk to my people on one condition...They paid to cater the food!

NOTES

CHAPTER 14
CUSTOMER SERVICE TRAINING/CUSTOMER COMPLAINTS

"The goal as a company is to have customer service that is not just the best, but legendary."
Sam Walton

One of the best investments you can make is teaching your people good customer service skills. This begins when you hire. You need employees that are smart, friendly, bubbly, like to talk and like to deal with people. Take a great personality like that, teach them to sell and solve customer problems and you are set. Customer service is the most important thing to increase sales and profit. Here are some points to help:

Always keep your promises to your customers. Your reputation is invaluable. Under-promise and over-deliver.

Answer your phone by the third ring and have a friendly voice answering it. Only have smart, friendly people that want to be there answering your phones.

Train your staff to listen to customers from their point of view not from the companies.

Teach them to handle customer complaints as they occur if they cannot call a supervisor as soon as possible. Have a toll free number posted in your lobby or showroom so customers can call if they are not 100% satisfied.

Go the extra mile for a customer even if it is not profitable at that minute. It will pay off down the road.

If a customer is upset have some gift cards ready to give them or give them a discount, free delivery, etc.

Post happy customer testimonials.

Three companies you can go observe or do more research on that have great reputations for customer service are:

a. Disney

b. Nordstrom

c. Lord & Taylor

CHAPTER 15
KNOW THE JARGON/BUSINESS DICTIONARY

"To be great in business, you must speak the language of business."
------Craig Thompson

Here is a short compilation of most common business terms. This is not even a small percentage of all business terms. The best source to go to is www.businessdictionary.com. The site always has a great word term of the day.

A
A.B.A.: American Bar Association or American Bankers
Association. This is a good place to get a lawyer referral.
ABC Method: An Accounting Term. It assigns AB or C to items of higher dollar values/more importance. Of course A would be most valuable assets.
Acquisition Cost: Total Cost to buy a property or business including costs.
Act of God: Damage caused by earthquake, tornado,
flood, etc. may not be covered by insurance.
Ad Valorem Tax: A tax based on value.
Amortization: Gradual paying of a debt.
A.P.R.: Annual Percentage Rate. Required on most loan documents.
Arbitration: Settling a dispute with an arbitrator rather than in a court of law.

Arms length transaction:
A transaction with both parties act in their own best interest. A sale between family members would not qualify.

Assignment of Income: Directing income earned by you
to be paid to another person for federal/tax purposes. This has proven risky by many taxpayers.

Audit: A full inventory of all items in your business. Also
involves reconciling all invoices, checkbook and cash counting.

B
Bait and Switch Advertising: When a company
advertises a product to "bait" customers into responding then not having that product or talking about how bad that product is. This is against federal and some state laws.

Balance Sheet: Your companies' financial position at the
end of an accounting period. Includes assets, liabilities and stockholder equity.

Base Rent: In a shopping center lease, example: base
rent of $18,000 per month plus 2% of all sales revenue over $75,000 per month.

Basis Point: One 100th of 1%. Accounting/Mortgage
term.

Bilateral Contract: A contract that requires both side to
perform certain duties.

Board of Directors: Group elected by shareholders to

run a corporation.

Board of Equalization: A government entity that does property tax assessments.

Bond: A certificate serves as evidence of a debt.

Business day: A day for conducting business, not a weekend or legal holiday.

C

CAM: Common Area Maintenance of a condo complex or
in an office building or shopping center

Capital Asset: Your company, your house, investments,
land, stocks & bonds, bank accounts are capital assets.

Capital Loss: When you lose money selling a capital
assets.

Cash Flow: Gross Amount/New Money

C.B.M.C.: Certified Business Coach

CC & R: In a condo or homeowners' association these are the rules and restrictions.

C.E.O: Chief Executive Officer. All employees report to the C.E.O.

C.F.O.: Chief Financial Officer. Runs the Finance Department and Reports to the C.E.O.

C.L.C.: Certified Life Coach

COBRA: Federal program which allows former employees to keep their health insurance in effect when they leave the companies.

COGS (Cost of Goods Sold): Basic Accounting principle.

This is your expenses. An example is what is the total cost for Ford to build a car.

C.O.O.: Chief Operating Officer. Runs the day to day operations of the company and reports to the C.E.O.

C.P.A.: Certified Public Accountant is a licensed accountant required to have additional training than regular accountant.

C.R.M.: Customer Relationship Management. A system of analyzing customer sales data. It is valuable to all sales organizations. It helps to target sales to the correct consumers.

C.S.R. : Customer Service Representative.

D

Davis Bacon Act: A federal law if you do a federal contract you must pay workers local prevailing wages.

Department Store: A large retail store with many sections/departments with combined sales over $10,000,000.00

Demographics: In marketing, this is a way to target certain age, income level, etc. portions of the population.

D.M. (District Manager): An executive responsible for a district of stores/offices. Store/Office managers report to a district manager.

D.O.C. (Department of Corporations): A state agency

Dock Height: Referring to a building with a loading dock. It is usually a warehouse.

Double Entry Accounting: Keeping business records where debits/credits are done with each transaction.

D.R.E.(Department of Real Estate or Division of Real Estate): A state agency regulating real estate brokers.

Dunn & Bradstreet: Think of this as the credit reporting agency for businesses.

E

Earnings & Profits: Earnings are your total revenue/Sales profits are what is left after expenses.

Early Retirement: Retiring before age 59 ½ may result in reduction of retirement benefits.

E-Commerce: The buying and selling of goods and services over the internet.

E.F.T.S. (Electronic Funds Transfer System): A digital system to move funds without the use of paper checks.

E&O Insurance: Errors & Omissions Liability Insurance.

This is a policy available to various professions like insurance or real estate companies. It protects the company/consumer in occurrence of negligence or omission of facts.

E.S.O.P. (Employee Stock Ownership Plan): Employees own all or part of a company.

Excel: Popular accounting spreadsheet program available from Microsoft.

Exempt Employee: Usually members of management also known as salaried, non-hourly employees. There is not overtime pay required in most states for these employees.

F

Fair Competition: Legal term establishing competitors to drive down costs for consumers.

F.D.I.C. (Federal Deposit Insurance Corporation):

Federal agency that guarantees funds in banks that are part of the Federal Reserve.

FICO Score: A number between 300-850 developed by
the Fair Isaacs Company used by credit bureaus and lenders to determine a consumers' credit worthiness.

FMLA (Family and Medical Leave Act): Federal law that only applies to company with 50 or more employees to provide leave to employees for certain medical or family reasons. Some states also have similar laws you will have to follow.

Fixed Expenses: They are unlike variable expenses such as utilities. Fixed expenses are constant regardless of sales. Your building rent is the same each month regardless of sales.

G

GAP Loan: Also called a bridge loan, mostly used by developers in the time of construction while it is still being sold or rented.

GM: General Manager

G.S.M.: General Sales Manager

Golden Parachute: Payout when a top executive leaves the company.

Goodwill: The value of a companies' name and reputation.

Goods & Services: Revenue Sources of Companies

Green Card: A card given by the United States government to immigrants that allow them to work legally in the United States.

Gross Income:
Take Total amount earned and minus the costs of goods to get gross income. Deduct total expenses from gross income to get net income/profit.

H

Hard goods: Also called durable goods. This is televisions, furniture, etc. Items built to last more than three years.

Hazard Insurance: A policy to provide protection against fires, storms, vandalism, etc.

Highest & Best Use: Real estate appraisal terms. Is the land or building being used in a way to produce the most possible net return?

H.O.A. (Home Owners Association)

Housing Starts: An important economic indicator of future growth. One of 12 indicators used by most economists compiled by the U.S. Department of Commerce.

HRM (Human Resources Management): New term for personnel department. Goal is to handle recruiting, pay rates, benefits and terminating employees. Also retention is part of HR.

I

Incentive Pay: A pay plan that gives an employee extra pay based on productivity above a certain level.

Independent Contractor: A contractor that is self-employed.

Index of Leading Indicators: A group of financial data used to see where the U.S. Economy is heading. This includes: the unemployment claims that week, new business orders, new business formations, new home starts among others.

Industrial Park: An area zoned and designed for manufacturing and warehouses.

IPO (Initial Public Offering): A corporation first public sale of stock.

J

Job description: A printed definition of a specific position including all the requirements to ensure that you hire the right person for the job.

Jobber: A wholesaler or middleman

Jointly and Severally: Legal term meaning they may go after you or against everyone signing the contract.

Judgment Lien: Court order placing a lien on a debtor's Property. Acts as an encumbrance on the property until the debt is paid.

JIT (Just In Time) Inventory: Also called the Toyota

Production System. It is an efficient inventory method that saves on warehouse costs by only ordering supplies as needed.

Justified Price: Fair market value an informed buyer will pay.

K

Key Person Life Insurance: An insurance policy places on their top executives. The company is protected from the unexpected death or permanent disability of key managers.

Kickback: An illegal practice. Payment secretly made to direct contracts or business to a company that may not deserve it.

Kiosk: An independent stand selling merchandise or advertising services popular in shopping malls.

Knockoff: A low price imitation of a name brand product. Not illegal like a counterfeit item is.

L

Labor Force: Total number of workers 16 years or older that are employed or seeking employment.

Laissez-Faire: A doctrine that wants little government interference in business and economic matters.

Leverage: Ability to take a smaller amount of money and borrow more to increase possible returns. Example if you have only $100,000 you cannot buy a $1,000,000 property but if you put the $100,000 as a down payment and borrow $900,000 you have just leveraged your $100,000.

LLC (Limited Liability Company): A business entity that provides some limited personal liability

List Price: Suggested Retail price designed by a manufacturer. You may sell above or below this price.

M

Mailing list: A compilation of names and addresses that can be sorted by age, sex, income level. used in email or direct mail companies for marketing.

M.B.A. (Master of Business Administration): Graduate degree

M&A: Mergers and Acquisitions

Mission Statement: A company's philosophy that guides how it does business.

Multifunction Device: A combination office machine including fax, printer, scanner and copier.

N

NAFTA (North American Free Trade Agreement)

NASDAQ : Along with the New York Stock Exchange, two of the largest exchanges for stocks in the world.

NOI (Net Operating Income): Income of a company or property after operating expenses have been deducted but before taxes and debt service.

New York Stock Exchange: See NASDAQ

Nonrecurring Charge: A one time expense or write off

also called an extraordinary charge. An example would be repairs from a fire.

O

Occupancy level: Also vacancy rate. Percentage of currently rented units. Usually hotels need a 60% occupancy rate to break even. Office buildings, apartments and shopping centers need an 80% or higher % to break even.

OEM (Original Equipment Manufacturer): Example, if you need a new Rim for your car you can buy an OEM part from the dealer or you can buy aftermarket.

Off the Balance Sheet: Not always illegal. If allowed you can lease rather than buy and future lease obligations can be kept off the balance sheet. Consult your C.P.A.

Owner-Operator: Refers to any business but is very popular with truckers. Many of them are owner-operators of their trucks.

P

P.A. : Professional Association; Personal Assistant;

Production Assistant

Perks: Special privileges for executives such as use of corporate jet, club memberships, etc.

P&L Statement: A statement of a company's profits and losses.

P.M. : Project Manager

Positive Cash Flow: Before tax cash flow much better than negative cash flow.

P.U.D. (Planned Urban Development): A planned mixed use community usually involving retail and multi-housing

Public Relations (PR) : Form of communication aimed at image building

Q

Qualified Prospect: A buyer with money and the authority to make the purchase.

Quasi-Public Corporation: Usually a public utility company

Quitclaim Deed: A document used to claim or transfer ownership to an interest in real estate transaction

R

Raised Check: A check with the amount and other information raised above the smooth surface to prevent alterations.

RM: Regional Manager, A VP level in some companies, regional managers have district managers that report to them.

R.O.I. (Return on Investment): Example, you spend $2,000.00 on direct mail if you get $1,600.00 in new business that is a great R.O.I.

RAM & ROM (Read only memory): Amount of memory on a computer but not storage space that is RAM memory.

S

S&P 500: The 500 most widely held stocks.

Salary: Regular, weekly, biweekly compensation not hourly.

S.E.C. (Securities & Exchange Commission): A federal regulatory agency (As a Florida gator fan I understand to many of you SEC means the Southeast Conference, Go Gators!)

Skimming: Illegal practice of failing to account for some sales to defraud a partner or the government.

Soft goods: Non-durable goods like textiles/clothing.

Spiff: An immediate bonus given to a salesperson by their employer or the manufacturer.

T

Tangible asset: This is your business machinery, furniture and the building. Not items for sale in inventory and not items with a life of less than one year.

Tax assessor: Official that determines property values relating to property taxes. These may be appealed but not with much success.

Total Loss: Damage so extensive it cannot be repaired or rebuilt back to original value.

U

Umbrella policy: increase liability coverage

Unfair competition: Untrue or unfair advertising, misleading consumers by imitating a competitor's package or trademark. Price dumping and sells into for less than the cost.

Utility Easement: Use of private property to lay gas, electric, sewer & water lines. In most cases, you cannot build over a utility easement.

V

Value Added Tax: A consumption tax added to a product during each stage of manufacturing.

V.P. Vice President: VP's report to the CEO, COO & CFO.

In most companies some businesses like banks name branch managers VPs. Stock brokerages name account execs VPs so they will be more impressive when meeting rich clients.

Example: You have two people waiting for you in your waiting room. One is called a sales rep., one is called a vice president. Who gets seen first?

W

Wilshire 5000: An index of stocks of the 5000 most common stocks.

Write-Off: Also call a write-down or charge off. The reduction of an uncollected debt or a drop in market price.

X

Xerox: A great example of branding people. Ask to make a Xerox even if they are using a cannon printer. Please pass the Kleenex is another example.

Y

YTD (Year to date): Related to sales, it is sales from day one of the fiscal year to that date.

Yield: Net rate of return on an asset or investment

Z
Zero sum game: Competition designed to destroy opposing party to leave them with zero.

Always improve your knowledge. Make sure to check out www.businessdictionary.com

CHAPTER 16
HIRING TOP MANAGERS/MANAGEMENT

"When you hire people that are smarter than you are, you prove you are smarter than they are."

------R.H. Grant

Hiring management would be a very big step for you as a small business owner that means that you are growing and that means you need someone to run another location or that you need someone to run a department or an office while you are away. This is a big step but also a very important decision if you run a department or run an office, it's yours, you're not going to steal from yourself, you are always going to try to make a sale, you're always going to try to help the customers. That might not be always the case when you hire a manager.

So, you need to be very careful when you hire. You need to make sure that you get someone very good, very good personality, someone very frugal with your money, someone that is going to work as hard as you would if not harder, someone that is going to take care of your customers and grow to help you make money and not steal from you.

The good thing about hiring a top manager is it will fill you up to think big picture thing to help your business expand, it will help you open up another location, which will double your income stream. And On certain occasion you can get someone that is better than you, has more experience than you and will actually do better than you would have done on the same position because of their experience, personality, education or a combination of all those.

Starting with that premise, let's start at the beginning as far as how do you get, how do you find, and how do you hire these managers that you're going to need to expand your business. In most small businesses, the first manager position would either be a sales type management or an office manager. Either one is a unique position as far as they are going to be reporting directly to the owner. Their job description has to be very flexible as far as they may have to be if there is an office person you might also want to cross train them on sales so that they can either cover vacation or sick days or help out on the sales floor when need it.

If there's a sales manager let them understand that as one of your first employees or one of your managers you expect them to do what is needed, whether it be help work at the warehouse, make deliveries, clean up, basically whatever is needed so make sure that you get someone that is willing to do that before they even take the position.

First, let's figure out how to actually find a manager. The best way to find a manager is by hiring someone that is already doing that job for someone else that you know for a fact does a good job. If you used to be an executive at a chain of shoe stores and you saved up and started your own shoe store. Well one of your old managers or one of your former co-workers will definitely be a good candidate to come to work for you, once you get to the point where you're open a second location or you need a manager. They know the business, you know them, you trust them and you know they are successful. That would be a very good place to start.

Now if you don't have that situation the next would be networking through your Rotary, Toastmasters or any of your groups if they know of someone that is trustworthy and they recommend someone that is someone you'd want to get their resume and talk to. With the higher unemployment rate there are a lot of good qualified people that are out there that are looking for work.

So the least expensive places to advertise are Craigslist.org, job bulletin sites, you can get a free listing with the Veterans Administration for hiring a veterans and in some place you can get tax credit if you hire veteran. If none of those low cost options get you a good candidate then you can always go on your local business journal and your local Sunday paper and put in just a quick 3-5 lines ad stating the position, the area and you could put the salary range if you wish. But basically you just put the position and the experience you want and the area, you may get dozens of calls and you can actually do yourself a favor by writing down all of the requirements of the job and do a just brief phone interview with the person when they call.

First, make sure that they have a good phone voice, strong, friendly, a little bit of sense of humor and make sure that they are understandable. Then have your list with you and make sure that they have all of the things that you require before they even come in because why bother wasting your time interviewing the person when they don't have what you need. What are the things that can be on the list?

In one of my former positions whenever I would hire management and I needed someone that had an insured vehicle because travelling from one location to another was part of the job, they also have to do errands like going to the post office, Staples. Having an insured vehicle was definitely a requirement. Being 18 years of older is a requirement. I required that they have previous management experience. I also required that they do a pass a full background check, credit check and a driving record check because we deal with large sums of money and we want people that can be bonded.

Someone with a very checkered credit history is a little more apt to be tempted to steal than someone who doesn't owe tens of thousands of dollars in debt. Basically, I would list all of these requirements along with some of the smaller ones like have them work on Saturdays, be free from 9-6, if someone who is a college student that needs something part time they wouldn't be able to work the hours. It's not discrimination if it's a requirement of the job and if you have the same requirement for everyone.

You can't come out and say "Are you _____ religion? Because that religion does not allow you to work on Saturday." Don't be stupid, that is not an appropriate question. But if your company is open on Saturdays and that's a requirement of the job then basically all you do and say is " The job requires you to work on Saturdays, is that a problem?" Then they are the ones that can decide whether the job is appropriate for them based on their lifestyle, their home life, their religious life, their everything.

Some jobs you don't care if they have a car or not, you don't care if they come there on a bus, an airplane, train or helicopter. That's fine if you have an office where you don't care how they get there that's great. But if they need to move around, to go to different locations, if they need to be mobile then you can require that of the job. You are going to eliminate some good people sometimes but you need to make sure that the job gets done so make sure you have a nice list and make sure that you weed out the people that don't qualify before you meet them.

Now when you do meet with them make sure that you are prepared. They are probably going to have a resume but also have them filled out an application. If you don't have an HR Department, an employee leasing or an attorney that does an employment application for you, those are something that you can get from Staples in packets. Make sure that those are legal in your state. But if you have them filled out an application along with the resume then make sure to look it over and kinda know a little bit about their background and have some questions in mind based on the application when you're meeting with them.

The things that you look for in a manager are different than what you are looking for in an employee. You will look for someone professional, dress appropriately, someone that makes eye contact, someone that is not overly shy, someone that is confident, and have a command presence but is not cocky or obnoxious about it. You want to have an interview questionnaire as a guideline but you really want the person talking.

You want to do more listening than talking. What you want to do is what you want to hear is how they manage because everyone has a different management style and if someone is too laidback then their people are not going to produce as much as they could as if they have someone that will keep them in line and push them. But if someone is too overbearing then the good employees will not work with them and you will have constant turnover or they will go overboard and that will lead to lawsuits and also lead to complaints with the labor board and it's just a lot of nonsense. You want someone that is in the fine line, they still want to work for you but they know they still have to do their job.

So you want to hear stories about how they have handled certain employees, you want to know if they have counseled employees, there should be an escalating procedures that they should be used to such as verbal warnings first time if someone does something, a written counseling statement or a written warning the second time and the third time is more depending on the offense that would lead to suspension, termination, etc.

But you want someone that has fired people before in the state you live in so that they are familiar with the local laws. You also want someone that has managed salespeople, managed some administrative people and managed blue collar workers. This will enable you to have someone that can be put in a few different departments, in charge of a few different departments and also that you should know they are flexible and that they have a good background.

Make sure that when you ask the questions that you like the answers that you get and that they sound smart and concise. A good manager is going to tell you how they have cut expenses, save money for the company, how they have raised profits, how they have increased sales and you basically want someone that is frugal and knows how to do projections/sales projections, knows how to meet a budget, knows how to recruit and hire people. You are going to want somebody that knows how to do marketing, knows how to get you leads and has dealt with vendors and suppliers.

It's not always necessary that they are in the exact same field you are. If you're an electrical contractor then they don't have to be an electrical contractor to be able to come to be your manager, they could have worked for a plumbing contractor, they could have worked for a builder or a pool contractor. Basically if they are in the same similar type of business, a lot of the steps and things that they're doing are similar. But if you're an electrical contractor having a florist might not be the best choice but if they're got a great personality and a lot of managerial experience doesn't mean they can't do the job they just might have a longer learning curve than someone that's in a little bit more similar industry.

As far as leads, if all they've ever done is used direct mail or telemarketing, one website that I've used and have successes with is servicemagic.com. The leads are not very expensive and I do have success with them, they are really good for supplying leads to service businesses like kitchen remodelers, landscapers, wedding planners and photographers. But they also do professional services they provide leads to builders, architects, realtors, roofers and 100 different type of industries they supply leads. It might not be the best way you might want to get business but some business are better than none. They charge different for each lead. But basically it's not too expensive it may be a few $1Ks for some of the leads and a few hundreds for others. If you don't have a lot of business when you first start until you get going and when you are slow down the road this will be something that even if you have to pay for the lead it is still better than nothing. So I would still recommend that.

But the main thing you have to look for when hiring a sales manager is you want someone that you are going to have confidence in. Basically this is going to be the answer guy, this is going to be the guy that can handle things when things are not going well, get someone that will blow you away, someone that you have a lot of confidence in right from the start. As far as pay I still recommend that if someone is going to have a $100K compensation package I only want 50% of that as base salary, I want the rest to be a car allowance or mileage, then I want quarterly/yearly bonuses based on production. Make them earn the rest of it. You give them a big fat salary then all of a sudden they just kick back and just relax.

I will tell you something that I will tell you in one of the later chapters but a manager cannot steal money from you unless you give the power to do it. You should be the one signing the checks, not your accountant, not your manager, not your lawyer. You should be the one signing the checks. If you want to give them some kind of credit card with a small credit line to buy purchases where you want to have a petty cash fund that is fine because you need that. But those checks should be signed by you, the money in the bank should only be controlled by you. It will make it a lot harder for people to steal from you if you're the only one that has control of your money, remember that!

CHAPTER 17
MOTIVATING EMPLOYEES

"Really great people make you feel that you, too, can become great." --------Mark Twain

"Success is not final, failure is not fatal, it is the courage to continue that counts."
-------Winston Churchill

One of the toughest jobs for any owner or manager is keeping your people motivated. But most psychologists and executives have come to the conclusion that you really cannot motivate anyone that does not want to be motivated. So you really what you need to do is you need to direct them and need to find what their button is and push that to get the most out of them.

But to get the most out of someone you need to start with a good employee to start with. A lazy or a bad employee even if the best motivator is not going to be able to make them into a good employee all they can do is to make them not as bad. So starting with good people is the first step. But let's just stick with motivating your existing employee to get the most out of them so that whatever business you do if you get the most out of your employees that is one of the keys to increasing profit and good customer service which leads to future business.

Money is a motivator for some people but not for others. You really have to know your people but basing the sales compensation packages of your people with some kind of incentive for increased sales or budget cutting or some kind of bonus program is still a good way to keep people working harder. So money may not be a main motivator for some people but it is for others. So still use it. Some manufacturers will have what is called as manufacturer spiffs, where if you sell their brand of product the employee can get $50 or $100. This can be good but be careful to make sure that your people are not just pushing product lines to get the spiffs but they are actually selling the best product for the customer.

Machiavelli said "it is better to be feared than loved." Fear can be a motivator but it is only temporary, If you constantly use the "I'll fire you if you don't do this" card it will not get you very far. Only threaten to fire someone if everything else fails and it's to the point where you don't mind if being tough on this person is going to make them quit because you are close to firing them anyway. When you get to this card make sure that you are ready to use it. If the employee improves then ease up on them. Only use the fear card as a last resort.

You can't go by what motivates you as a gauge as to what motivate your people. Some of your people are going to be motivated by doing a good job, some of them are going to be motivated by place, some of them are going to be motivated by motivating factors like personal growth, advancement, promotions, prestige. Some are going to be motivated by security, some are going to be motivated by recognition, getting plaques going on trips. Just because something works on you doesn't mean it works on them. Make sure you know your people and you use that.

Your people all have certain goals. Make sure that you know what their goals are and show them how they can get them by doing a good job. There's a saying that you get more with honey than with vinegar. If you're the kind of boss that all you ever do is downgrade your people, yell at them and talk about when they do something wrong you're going to have a tough time motivating your people. They're only going to do enough to not get fired, they're not going to do extra for you. You've got to find them, catch them do something right and when they do give them a giftcard, recognize them in front of their co-workers. Do something to recognize them. Make sure that they enjoy working for you.

What you can do is you can actually gear your company policies towards helping you: 1. Motivate your people and 2. Move your numbers. I remember at a financial services company I ran, I was always very competitive with the other district, the other sets of stores and we used to come up with different ways to use the rankings of all 20 offices to motivate our people.

So we tweaked it, we did things like usually the top 3-4 managers will go on a nice trip to Vegas each year. But we want to expand it so where we made it where the top store will get lunch, then we change it to where the top five will get lunch, and the top number one store will also get gift card. We just made it where if you are in the top five or the top 10 you are always going to get something so it gives more incentive. We also made it where the bottom stores have to pay, where they actually have to send a check to the winners. So we kinda made it like a double edged sword, where we really gave them an extra incentive to do well but where we also made it to really hurt if you are on the bottom because you not only were embarrassed that you are at the bottom but you also have to pay money to the winners.

This goes by my saying where you always want to have winners because winners always find a way to win. But you want people that more than want to win because most people want to win, you got to get people that hate to lose. That if they lose once it's going to leave a bad taste in their mouth that they're going to do whatever they have to so that the next month/quarter they will not be down there that they will be winning. So try to adjust your company policies/procedures to help you motivate people.

Some of the other things that you need to do to help motivate your employees is that you need to spend time talking to your employees and find out what's going in their lives, what they're up to, what motivates them. If you have employee that loves music you can use that. If you have an employee that is a crazy sports fan and your company has seats to the local sporting team, then give them tickets if you're not using them. That would be a great incentive. Reward them when they do something well, reward them then and don't do it six months from now. Reward them, do it in a conference call. Communications is very important.

Whenever I manage multiple locations and I would travel around to my different stores but sometimes I couldn't get there to each one for weeks, or months but every Monday morning they would all dial in, and I would have a conference call and we would get over latest memos, latest announcements, we would welcome new people, we would talk about problems we are having. Basically it is just a good way to communicate and to recognize people. You can always do an e-mail blast and let people know who is doing great. But when you actually say it in front of their coworkers or in the conference call or in the manager's meeting or something like that then that is something that people like and they actually appreciate it.

Celebrate their birthdays, send them a birthday card, let them know that you care about them, that's part of motivation. They want to know that you look at them as an important part of the business. So if they have special skills then delegate some projects to them. Make them feel that they are important to the company and they will do better for you. If you have customers that sends in letters or call to say you're employee is doing a good job, then use that to recognize them. If you have promotions you can do a little free article and a picture and put in a local newspaper/business journal as recognition or thing. Do what you can to recognize good employees so that you keep them.

Remember my saying as far as employees; I want my people to be very very happy or very very nervous. Part of the thing to keep them very very happy is review your company benefits, if you're not competitive if you don't have 401K or dental plans like other companies have you could lose good people to that. It's also something that they're not going to look at your company as long term. If you don't have a 401K plan and your competitors do they're going to look at your competitors as a more long term solution. So look at those things and just look at everything that is involved in your employee's job and see what you can do that is affordable to improve their job situation because the happy they are the happy they are at work the more they will treat better the customers and the more profit you are going to make.

CHAPTER 18
TERMINATING EMPLOYEES

"If you cannot change your people.....change your people."

------Unknown

This is by far one of the most stressful and worst part of being a business owner or manager and that is firing or terminating employees. Firing people is never pleasant, can be very stressful but many times it cannot be avoided. Most of the time, you as the boss do not fire someone they fire themselves by their actions or their lack of performance.

There are some things you need to do make sure that it is done appropriately so that you avoid legal issues that can cost the company a lot of money. Never fire someone when you are angry. No matter what they do, if they're drunk, you caught then stealing if you fire them when you are angry you are emotional, you are going to say things that you may or may not mean, you are not going to have all your paperwork in order and that is going to hurt you.

So the best thing to do when you are angry when you find something you can still fire them but it doesn't hurt to send them home, suspend them, get their keys to the office, make them count their cash drawer, their cashier or if they have some kind of responsibility for money. Count their money, get their keys, do a written counseling statement or reprimand stating that you are going to fire them without pay for two days, five days over how many days it will take to get everything ready.

Just put the highlights of what happened but don't go into it because it's just going to get you more emotional and just get them out of there. Suspend them but don't fire them when you're angry.

Make sure that you have a company policy manual. Use that to give you legal grounds to fire someone. If you don't have one that is not always necessary and not every situation will be covered. Gross negligence, insubordination, repeated tardiness, theft, abusive to customers are all grounds that you have legal standing to fire regardless whether it is in your policy manual. But you want to make sure that you have a policy manual, and have your attorney look it over to make sure that it complies with your local, city, state and federal labor laws and OSHA laws. If there is a union you want to make sure that it is compatible with your CBA collective bargaining agreement.

You need to document everything, you need to be truthful. You need to keep it to the actual conduct or performance, you can but it wouldn't be smart to use personal reasons to fire someone. Keep it business, keep it professional but make sure you have a document. Do a written reprimand or a discharge letter stating the reasons why they are being terminated and hopefully you have prior verbal and written proof that you've tried to fix this conduct in the past.

Not always do they have to have a pattern sometimes it's something they can do that is so gregious that you have the right to fire them right then and there. Make sure you have a witness. Don't meet up with them in private because they can make up things that you did or didn't say. Make sure you have someone preferably from HR but you might not have an HR rep but make sure there's another manager or another person there. Just make sure that it's not a person that is involved in any kind of incident. Like if they have a fight with an employee make sure that the other employee they had a fight with is not your observer.

Be respectful, be professional, and keep it short. It doesn't have to be long explanation, keep it to the facts, keep it only to what you can prove not what you think. If you think they stole money but you can't prove it then just go with the facts. Go with the fact that they are responsible for the money, go for the fact that this amount of money is missing that they're responsible and that whether it was stolen by them or it got misplaced or stolen by someone else because they left it unattended or unlocked. Either way it's gross misconduct, and either way your money is gone, their member of management or their member is responsible for the money.

Keep it short, stick to the facts and make sure that when you let them go that you get all the company properties such as keys. You still may want to consider changing your locks and your alarm codes. Change those but make sure to get company property. Give them time to clear out their office. This is a smart thing to do but in most state this is a legal requirement, make sure you have a final paycheck including the last day that they work. If you fire them at 10 in the morning in some states they are required to be paid 8 hours for that whole day. So make sure that they get a check stub but make sure that you get a signature from them stating that they got their check stub so that they can't complain to the state that you didn't pay them for their last day of employment.

Don't give them a hug, don't shake their hand, don't wish them well, just be professional and get them out of your location as soon as possible. There will be some people that will not act professional, they will threaten you, they will try to key your car, they will try do different things such as throw a brick through your window. That's why you have insurance. Park your car up the street for a couple of days. Just be professional, once you've done a couple of this it gets easier. It is never a fun thing but just remember that they have every opportunity to change their behavior or improve their performance and they couldn't do it. Some people are better off or some bad employees are better off working for your competition and running their numbers to the ground and hurting their profit instead of hurting yours.

One of my former bosses has this thing where he would say that it's better to look at someone in the eye and say" You know this isn't working, I think you'll be happier someplace else." In a lot of cases, that is the truth. Just make sure that you are protected by documenting everything and making sure that you have a witness present so that it's not your word against theirs.

CHAPTER 19
ACCOUNTING AND SALES PROJECTION

Accounting is definitely one of the least exciting topics in running a business but it is one of the most important. If you don't keep track of your money you don't know if it's lost. If you don't keep track of your money, you're going to lose your business because the IRS will shut you down. If you don't keep track of your money, who is going to?

Of course you're going to have a CPA but this CPA is not going to be working for you. It's up to you and your employees to keep track of expenses, to keep receipts and to keep books. It doesn't matter if you just have an old-fashioned ledger of expenses and invoices, and cash on hand or if you use a computerized system. Most people use a computerized system like Quick books and they have a bookkeeper that keeps track of the checkbook and keeps track of everything. But the main parts of accounting are the same whether you do it computerized or if you have a bookkeeper or do it by hand.

The main thing is to have a main system set up, to have all of your financial records, your invoices, checks, anything you spend on your business and all of your incoming receivables all of them have to be documented immediately so that you know exactly what's coming in, what's going out at all times. You need to make sure that you know exactly how much money you have in the bank, you need to know what your inventory is at all times, you need to know how much is coming in the next 30-60 days, you have to know how much your monthly bills are whether its salaries, rents, things like that, those are all the basic principles that you need to do to make sure that your business accounting runs smoothly.

Some of the other issues you need to look at is payroll has to be done. That is the legal requirement that you can't get around. You have to pay your rent on time, if you want to stay good with your landlord and if you want to be able to have a place to operate and to make sure that they are going to renew your lease. Most companies find that it's easier to do payroll every two weeks instead of weekly. Some states you're not allowed to do monthly so every two weeks is by far the most popular.

If you want to do your own payroll there are step by step instructions on state IRS and IRS.gov sites on deductions. The Quick book applications will do all that for you as far as deductions that you need to take out for withholding taxes, social security and all that type of thing. So doing the actual payroll is time-consuming but it's not too bad once you've done it a few times. Most people use some kind of payroll service where basically they will handle that.

Now as far as inventory, inventory is something you need to make sure you stay on top of. You or someone you trust implicitly need to stay on top of this because this is where theft can occur. You also need to make sure that the inventory is locked and secured at all times. You also need to have some kind of PAR system. Basically you set a par level on how many of these items are supposed to be in stock so that when you get down to a given level then you automatically need to order this many on your next incoming shipment. (Eg: I think you should have 6 of this stock at all time and once you get down to 6 you automatically know you need to order this many on your next incoming shipment.)

You need to make sure that anything wasteful spending like overtime is eliminated. So make it a policy that overtime can only be in an emergency and only with the next level of supervision approval first. You can get a time clock from Staples or Office Depot to keep your time. If you have multiple locations and you have all your locations have access to a computer another easy system that I have had experienced with that works very well that is online timekeeping system that is computerized. It is called paycom.net and they are a pretty good company to work with.

When you first set up they will do a web conference and a training webinar to teach you how to use their system. It is very user friendly, employees can go on and change their deductions, they can go in to clock in and clock out, they can print out their paycheck stubs online, they can change the numbers of exemptions they have, it's all password protected, each employee has their own password. As a supervisor if someone forgot to clock in or if you're doing a report on who's working in this location, how many hours, basically there are dozens and dozens of reports you can use for accounting and payroll management.

Another thing that you need to make sure you need to do is try to always pay your bills on time as soon as possible. There are some companies such as American Express with their open program, which is great for small businesses they can set up a lot of programs and so can your local bank, Mastercard or Visa where you get a lot of your receivables sent/direct deposit/wired right into your account instead of waiting for paper checks that would take longer and then you have to deposit that paper check. You can also look into electronic mean of deposit, one of the most common one is ACH, auto clearing house, where basically you get a paper check and you enter into a computer system and it's electronically debited immediately from your customer's account. Anything that you can do the quick and the money getting into your account is always a good thing. Look into taking Paypal and other online payment services is also a good way because a lot of customers are nervous about using their credit card but if they already have their paypal account then all they have to do is transfer it from their paypal account to yours and you get paid immediately.

Another thing to remember about accounting is that your accountant will set up certain procedures that you should definitely follow. Don't try to do anything that will jeopardize you, make sure you pay all of your required taxes, don't try to skim, don't try to have a second set of books, it's not worth it. It's better to just do everything in the up and up and pay what you are required to pay even though it might hurt. Don't try to get an accountant that is too edgy, trying to do too many risky deductions that can hurt you because even though the accountant is recommending it you are the one that signs, you are the one that is responsible.

Just like with your attorney or just like with anything else your accountant cannot steal from you unless you give them the power to sign checks. It's a lot harder for someone to take your money if you don't give them access. If you are the only one to sign your checks that make it a lot harder for them to steal from you.

Another area that has to do with financial part is sales projections. Sales projections in Year 2,3-10 are a lot easier because you have the prior year to base your sales on. What a lot of companies do is they will take the prior year and then the month before and they will merge those and do a projection. Most companies conservatively want at least 2-5% increase in sales from the prior year's sales. The exception would be from prior year would be a record year then maybe just beat it or just matching that would be a good thing.

Another thing is when you do projection is you have to look at other factors that can affect sales. If the city has got the street torn up in front of your location and customers can barely in and out it is very unlikely that you'll get the same amount of sales this month for this time as you did last year when there was no construction and it was easy to get in and out of the location. You always have to use common sense when you do sales projection. If you don't have a prior year sales to go by you can rely on your knowledge of the business if you use to run the same type of company that you now own and you know about what an average sales per month is but with the brand new location that is probably unrealistic because it is hard to gauge how much business is going to come in.

Except you can go by with what you plan on marketing. If you plan on doing 10,000 pieces of mail and you know in your area the average return is 3% return rate that means you are going to have 30 customers that are going to come in that month from your mailing and your average sales is $1,000 then basically what your closing percentage is let's say it's 50% that means that you'll have 15 sales out of those 30 and your average sales is $1,000 that means you can project $15,000 in sales.

Basically your first year of sales projection are going to be based more on what you expect to come in from your marketing plan. Then you are going to go with a closing percentage and then times that by the averages sales that you have in your company. From these you also take all of your expenses, your rent, your salaries, what your supplies cost and you'll deduct these too and so you will not only have your projected sales but your also going to have your projected expenses and you are going to have your projected profit. So try to work on this, and improve this and fine tune this each month and after your 12th month you'll have a whole year trend to see what months are good, what months are bad, what months are not as good, you might want to increase advertising on those months to even it out and on the busy months you might need to gear up and hire some part time help/part time employees.

This is what sales projections are for so you can plan ahead. After the 13th month you'll be able to use the month before and the 12 months before to combine the two, average the two and then you'll have a good projections for the next year. But always try to push your people to keep in mind meeting next year is not what you want, you always have to beat the year before unless there are extenuating circumstances.

CHAPTER 20
RISK MANAGEMENT/CRISIS MANAGEMENT

Risk management and crisis management are MBA words, big business words that basically can be summed up like this. Risk management is preparing for bad things and by planning ahead you minimize the damage and the cost that could have happened. Crisis management is how you handle something bad that happened and how to minimize the impact and to get yourself back in business as quick as possible.

Risk management is why you have insurance, risk management is why you have a security guard, and risk management is why you have an alarm company. If you see one of the employees mopping the lobby risk management is teaching them and giving them the tools to put a "wet floor" sign so customers doesn't come and slip and fall and sue you. If you see an employee climbing on the chair to reach something on the top shelf, risk management is why you have a ladder to teach them how to use it properly so you that don't have a workman's comp claim when they fall and hurt themselves.

Basically, it's just like when a parent baby proof a house when they have a toddler so that the child doesn't get into the chemicals and swallow some poison or put their hands in an electrical outlet, that's the way to look at your business. You have to look at any potential hazards for customers or employees and eliminate as many of them as possible to lessen the chances of injury or death that could result in a loss of your company from lawsuits. If you see a cord running across an aisle way, where customers or employees could walk on it and trip, you re-route the cord up above if possible out of the way, hidden nice and neat or if you don't have time to do that then buy some duct tape or buy a rug, buy something to cover the cord until you can fix it properly but either way when you see a hazard you need to address it right then and there not wait till something occurs that is going to cost you money.

You need to be diligent and vigilant and always be looking for potential hazards and you need to train your employees to think the worst that could happen and try to think of solutions that could lessen those problems.

There are going to be some parts of this management that you are not going to have much choice with. State fire marshal/fire department comes in for inspection, of course you're going to check their id and call the fire department and make sure they are legit. If they are the real thing they have the right to come and inspect your establishment and you better have a fire extinguishers they better be up to date, there better be signs for fire extinguishers, there better be exit signs that glows in the dark or that are lighted when the power goes out, there better be exits, you can't keep someone lock in, they have to be able to get out in case of fire. There are going to be state, local and federal laws about safety and about risk management that you have to comply with. You also have to look at it from a business point of view, it's better to spend a few dollars in prevention than the lawsuits that happen when you don't plan ahead.

Crisis management is something that no matter how much you plan, I could not have planned when the underage driver borrowing her father's car hits the gas instead of the brake and smashed into my lobby causing over $20,000 in damage but because I have things in place and assistance in place things happen very quickly within hours we were operating again with boarded up window and within days because I already have vendors pre-selected and checked out and they came and got everything done within 2-3 days we have new glass, contractor came and did the repairs and we were back in business.

So crisis management is when something that happens, it could be a national disaster, it could be an earthquake, it could be a tornado, it could be a fire, it could be hurricane. We have a system in place where basically whenever something like that happens they know they need to call me right away so that I know that everything is okay there, everyone is all right or if something is wrong, are the computers down? Is the electric out? Is the power out? Is the water out? Is there a gas leak? So if I know that I have the list of all the utility companies in all my location, so if there's a power outage I can call the electric company and most of the time there's a recording that says "we know about it and we're on it" or if they don't know about it I let them know and then I get back with my people.

We also have redundancies where you need to have backup systems, all of our data has backup so if there's power outage or fire our data is offsite so that we don't lose all our important customer files and customer information and financial data so you have to think about all these and plan ahead. But one of the main thing in crisis management also is that you have to remain the calm and collected one because your people, the customers, the people that are affected they might become emotional and upset but you have to be calm and collected and get through it to get yourself back in business as quick as possible.

One of the things you can do beforehand is training, if one of your establishments gets robbed teach your people exactly what to do and the police department and fire department actually come in and do free training sessions for your people. One of the things you teach them is don't try to be a hero just cooperate give away the money but it doesn't mean that you can't have a system and place where they get less money.

We would have a system in place where the majority of the money is in the bank where it would come out as needed and we would only keep a few hundred dollars in the drawers in each of the tellers and cashiers so that there's less money to be taken in a robbery. You have to make sure that all of your procedures are followed which means that you have to check it because employees will do what you verify. What you checked on they're going to make sure they stay on top of so you have to make sure you stay on top of them.

But basically we have a system where if there's a robbery we taught them not to be a hero, to give up the money, to be cooperative, we had silent arm buttons that they could push so the police department would be on their way. But the first thing to do is call 911, report there is robbery, report that there's an incident, next would be to call the supervisor. Now if there's any kind of crisis that has to do with a lawsuit or something that happens with one of the major owners of the company, any kind of issues like that the media may approach your people, there may be reporters that call, you need to teach your people that they are not allowed to talk to the media, they are not allowed to talk on behalf of the company.

There should be one person as the spokesperson, most likely you as the owner of the company would be the company's spokesperson. Or you could have a public relations person acting as a company spokesperson. But basically whenever there's a crisis you want to make sure to be honest but you also want to consult with your business coach and more importantly your attorney to make sure that nothing you say by being honest is going to put yourself in jeopardy and open yourself up to lawsuits.

So you do want to answer any questions, and if it's appropriate to apologize then apologize but the main thing is if you made a mistake you need to make it right. One of the biggest crisis management issues that was handled correctly was Tylenol. They were pro-active, got all the pain medication taken off the shelves, did a great public relations job and recovered and grew even bigger. There are plenty of companies BP Oil as one of the most recent ones that did not do a very good job and it made it look like they were avoiding paying people, that they were covering things up and that they have something to hide. Basically, being honest is something that is always recommended but you also want to make sure that you get good advice and make sure you are not admitting to things that are not going to cost you later.

CHAPTER 21
SETTING UP OR IMPROVING YOUR WEBSITE

About 60% of businesses now have some type of web presence. There are many different types of websites you can do. Some are just a simple 2-3 pages of simple information that main goal is to explain a little bit about your company but mainly to direct your customers to a phone number or an e-mail to contact you for information. These are simple websites that are simple to run and set up. For businesses that are service oriented, these are probably all you will ever need.

If you want to step up your website you can set it up so that it is interactive and you can actually sell videos, you can actually sell products online using a credit card or pay pal and your website can actually generate you money at 2am when you are actually close and sleeping.

So let's just go over some basics of websites. First thing that you'll need when you do a website is you need to buy a domain name. They cost between $8 and $30 per year but the place I've always purchased my domain name for a pretty good price is godaddy.com. The next thing you'll need to do is you need to have a plan to build your site, you can actually build website with a lot of different software program that you can buy at Staples and Office Depot.

But the easiest thing would be to use one of the templates sites and the next thing you're going to need is you need a host, one that runs your site. The easiest company to do those through would be through

Vistaprint.com or GoDaddy.com or someplace like Yahoo, where you can actually just pay a few dollars amount and just use one of their templates site, they'll use the domain name that you already bought and then once you set it up, you pay a monthly fee and you keep it going and they'll host it for you.

If you want to do it yourself that's fine but it's a lot easier if you just use one of those companies. But when you build your site you need to have some things in mind when you build it from scratch. You need to know the different languages that your site is using, you have to know about html language, you need to make sure that your site is compatible with Mac and Windows, and you have to make sure it is compatible with the major browsers for Apple, Safari, Internet Explorer and also Mozilla Firefox is also becoming popular so it would be prudent to make sure that your website is visible in all those browsers because you don't want to lose business just because your website is not compatible with those browsers.

Another thing you might want to consider is that even though you may have broadband your customers still might be on dial-up, or on a slower DSL connection and if your website has a bunch of fancy graphics and flash images that look very impressive on broadband, if you get on there with a dial-up that could just take forever to load up and they may just get frustrated and click off. So make sure that if you do have a lot of flash or graphics that take up a lot of bandwidth that there's a button on the bottom that they can skip the intro or skip those and goes right to your text, which text part of your site does not use much bandwidth that they will be able to get on there fine.

Another thing I would recommend with the website is to consider whether you're going to have an information site or whether you want your site to actually bring you business and actually make you money because then you're going to want to consider having a website that people actually can find very easily so you're going to look at having a site and then also you want to pay extra to have your site listed with one of the marketing companies so that it comes up first on the first or second page when someone clicks in plumbers in your local area or real estate agents or architects if you pay extra to have your site marketed with Google and with other web hosts and some of the other search engines then you'll actually come up first.

If you're buried 15 pages down then you're going to have a tough time for people to click you.

Another thing you're going to want to make sure in your website is that you have the ability for people to purchase on your website. Most of the template sites have a cart option where people can shop on your site and then through them you'll be able to take credit cards and pay pal but if you don't use one of the template sites you'll have to go through your bank or your merchant service that you take credit cards with right now or you're going to have to go through pay pal, which is pretty easy to deal with.

If you go through pay pal you won't have to use anyplace else because pay pal people can use their credit card, they can actually do a check from their account or people can actually use their pay pal account itself without even having a bank account. So think about how the person is going to pay, think about how to make your site easier to locate by search words. Google by far is the largest but you also need to be listed with MSN, Mozilla Firefox and all the different search engines so that your website comes up first.

The other thing to remember about website is that it is still a marketing and advertising vehicle. So if you are required by law, if you are in a loan business, in a real estate business, if it's a medical, basically if you are licensed in any way or any of your employees are required to be licensed and if there's any disclosure on marketing then that still has to be present on a website. It doesn't have to be intrusive but basically at the bottom of each page there has to be a disclosure that this company or this person is licensed by the state board or whatever disclosure is that you need to have on any of your brochures or any written materials also has to be on your website. Just because it is out on the internet doesn't mean that you don't have the same state rules to go by and you don't want to get a fine by something stupid like not having the required disclosure on there.

CHAPTER 22
EXPANSION/M&A (MERGERS AND ACQUISITIONS)

Before discussing expansion let's discuss mergers and acquisitions briefly. Mergers and Acquisitions although used together they mean different things. Merger usually means a combination or combining of pretty much equal sized companies that usually agreed to become one. This could be a good thing, the little details that you have to make sure that you have are making sure you know what each company is worth what is called the asset valuation. You want the books looked over by the CPA so you know the cash flow. You want to know the cash valuation of the company and you want to know all of their assets.

A merger is usually a cash or could be a stock swap and normally it's not a 50-50 proposition. Normally, you have two owners and one of the owners is probably want to retire or step down that's why he's merging or if both businesses have come to the realization that they were able to grow stronger if they are one company because there's a lot of redundancy that they can probably eliminate. They probably don't need two vice president of sales you can just go down to one, you probably don't need to have as many administrative people in the total companies so there is probably some cost savings and there will probably be some cost savings by buying supplies in greater quantities.

You probably will not need to get into anti-trust issues but in some areas if you're the only two companies in the certain area there could be anti-trust issues as far as you have monopoly but that is something that you will barely run into a merger of two small companies but if you're larger, medium sized companies that could be something if you're in a county with 12 gas stations and you're merging with another company and you reach down 6 and you own every gas station in the county that could be an issue because you actually could control all of the fuel prices in the whole county where you reside, that will probably be the only type of situation where you run into that.

Normally in a mergers and acquisitions scenario, which we'll go into acquisitions first but in a merger scenario or in a partnership or in any kind of thing where you have another person involve with your business whether they're stock owner or investors or anything like that you're going to make sure that you as the owner and founder of the company maintain at least 51% ownership or stock. This will eliminate you becoming Steve Jobs or other people that have started companies and then got voted out because the stockholders are upset because they had a downtime or they don't like your ideas. If it's your company and you want to keep it 51% is the magic number.

Now if it comes to the point where you want to move on to something else then it doesn't matter except that if you have a lesser percentage you're not going to have control. If they run the company to the ground that 50%, 20% or whatever % you have left could end up being worthless.

Most of the time when you are merging one thing to remember besides the cash flow and the amount of the inventory and the amount of sales they do is you also have to look at what your business is worth it's called goodwill. Because a lot of business guys who own a business is your reputation. If you have a good reputation in the industry that is worth something, make sure that the company you're merging with also has this. You also have to make sure that both companies have the same type of corporate structure and culture and that they're going to work together. If you get a feeling that even though on one hand it could work but it's not going to work as far as personalities then it might be better to walk away.

As far as acquisition, acquisition is always talked about with mergers but it's actually not the same thing. Acquisition is when someone buying you. If you're about to retire that could be a great thing. If you have had your company for 20 years and now there's a big company or even another medium sized company that wants to buy your company then you can consider that an honor because if you didn't have a good company built up then no one would be interested in buying you.

In that case if you are looking to get out or maybe to step down an acquisition could be a good thing.

In some cases if you're a public company in the stock market it could be called what is called a hostile takeover, an acquisition that is not of your choice and basically if they have enough votes of stockholders they can vote to sell the company even against your will. That's where you want to make sure you have 51% of the stock but that is rare in small companies.

Another thing that happens with acquisitions that could be a good or bad thing is a lot of times a large company will come in and see a small or medium sized company that has definitely some potential and they think that with their acquisition the company can even perform better. A lot of times they don't want to come in and change things they like the way things are run. So they will come in and buy your company and actually wants to keep you on as running the company. So you can have the best of both worlds, you could make a huge payday potentially of millions of dollars, still get to run your company, maybe even still have a big portion of stock probably not the majority though since they are purchasing your company they'll probably have at least 51% but you could still have a large portion of your company and still have some say in how it's run but not the ultimate say like you used to but still get to stay and run the company but remember you're still going to have someone to report to now even if your title is CEO or President or whatever you're still going to have someone else to report to when you used to be the boss now you are the boss but you have someone at corporate to report to. Remember there is good and bad with that.

Now let's talk about simple business expansion. If you have some kind of manufacturing site, expansion could involve just adding square footage, adding more machinery, adding more employees, expansion could be making some of your products overseas because of the cost-savings. When you do that make sure that you go and visit where they are made so you don't have any PR issues with child labor or anything like that and also make sure that the quality is the exact same or as close as possible so that you can still keep your prices at the same level.

Now if you have other businesses, expansion can be a little bit more difficult. Let's say that you have a retail store and after all the payroll, all the taxes, all the supplies and all your expenses you make $30,000 per year profit at that location. That is not enough usually for you to want to quit your full time job or for you to be there full time. So $30,000 is not really that great so you would want to increase sales to increase that profit but if you keep the same profit level but you open two more locations and hire managers to run them and got your supplies from the same supplier then basically your three locations making $30,000 per year net profit would bring you a $90,000 per year profit.

So if you use that same math and have ten locations you're making $300,000. That's why expansion is always interesting and enticing to business owners that you can reproduce what you've done on one or two levels and basically the only thing that you're going to need to really grow is everything else stays the same all you need is maybe a bigger warehouse for warehousing and keeping the inventory and you might need to add unless it's outsourced more office help. You're going to have a lot more invoices that have to be paid, you're going to have a lot more things that need to be done as far as employee payroll and employee benefits and all that.

But if you are successful in one location you can just duplicate that over and over and you can still be successful. Most business owners usually can run up themselves until they get to 4 or 5 or 6 locations and after that you either need to have a manager running the office part and the owner would go and act as the regional or district manager to go into the locations or at some point if the owner wishes to stay back at the corporate office and look over long terms goals and look over the office then you need to look into having a district or regional manager that will be your eyes and ears and make sure that everyone is doing their job, the stores are clean, things are being done right, no one is stealing from you, so that would be one of the things that you need to look at once you get into the expansion.

Another thing you need to look at is once you have expanded into 8 or 10 stores you might find that instead of opening a new location, getting new furniture, getting new inventory, hiring new staff that you may be interested in actually expanding through acquisition. If you cost you $50,000 to open a new location and then business is slow the first 12 months until you build up a clientele there then maybe buying an existing location that's full of inventory, has an existing staff and already has built in clientele maybe buying a location that is already there would be more advantageous to you and will get you going quicker.

So when you consider an acquisition if you know the owner why not approach him and ask him for a price. He may not be interested in selling and you just move on and open up the location across the street from him and run him out of business. But a lot of times when you approach someone as far as acquiring their business you never know they may be very interested in just getting out especially if they just own 1 or 2 locations. There may be health issues, there may be all kind of issues that you're not aware of.

Another thing to consider also is if you acquire their business and then for the first year or two have them to continue do run the business and pay them as a manager that could also be a good move for you because there won't be much disruption as far as the customers, what they see will be the same. Then within that two years you could always bring in your own person and they can even be trained by the outgoing owner.

So mergers and acquisitions are always something that is going to come up once you get to a certain size. A lot of bigger companies that are going to try to buy you, they are going to try to make your purchase with stock or they are going to get financing through a bank. I personally know if an acquisition starts and it's financed there is a chance that the sale will not go through if the financing does not happen. So, just because you accept an offer and just because it looks like it's going to close don't count on it until the actual transfer is done because financing can fall through with the bank.

Unless it's a blue stock company I would not really be interested in a stock offer, cash is king and cash is the only thing that is 100% real as far as them buying your business. So be wary of stocks, don't count your eggs before they are hatched as far as the purchase deal and most companies are going to want you or require you to sign some kind of agreement that you are not going to open the same type of business within a certain number of years or ever in the immediate area of the business that you just sold. Don't think that's out of the ordinary because that is pretty standard.

They also are probably going to want you to sign some kind of agreement that if there's a lawsuit, sexual harassment suit, unemployment suit, any kind of lawsuit from a customer or from anyone that happens where the event happens before the closing of the sale that you're going to be the one responsible for that. Because they are going to take responsibility for everything that happens in the business let's say January 1st. But something that happens in December that would still when it was under your watch so you're still responsible for that. So that is also something that most companies are going to require when they buy. Consult your Attorney.

CHAPTER 23
YEARS 1, 5 AND 10

The first year of your business is actually the toughest and if you make it past year one which is if you're smart enough to educate yourself by reading books like this and others to make yourself as smart as possible you have a better chance. But in year one it is when your sales projection is based on more assumptions than track record, when you are probably the one doing the majority of all the work, you and maybe your spouse and maybe other parts of the family that are working for free or next to free. So in the first year of the business you're going to have to be willing to be the janitor, be the maintenance man, be the salesperson, be the gofer, be the painter, be the everything.

But once you have everything up and running and the business is starting to form itself you're going to have to start probably by the end of the first year definitely going into the second year to look at starting into hiring employees. When you bring on employees you're going to start looking into benefits and that's why employee leasing may be the easiest way to have a good benefit package for your employees and for yourself and not have to worry about doing all the payroll and not have to have the extra expense.

Some of the employee leasing company will even do everything even up to getting a workman's comp insurance. You can also start look into protecting your assets if you already don't have a business insurance, get it. A lot of your insurance companies that will also provide your homeowners insurance, and your car insurance will give you discount if you also do your business through them. This may be good and it may be a good savings but you really want a business insurance agent that not only specializes in business insurance but specializes in the type of business that you're in.

Now some of you may wonder why you'd have insurance when you're going to be leasing your facilities. Well the business insurance is also the one that protects if there's a robbery or if a break in or if your inventory burns up in the fire, some of the little things that insurance that may not be as obvious as if you have a leased building and there is a fire or some kind of incident where there's damages your insurance company may not or may say you're not covered because it's not on the interior of the building or it's not part of your inventory that it's actually the landlord's expense so you go to the landlord with the issue and the landlord will say no it's not my expense because you are on net lease and the damage was caused by blah...

So basically the landlord doesn't want to pay, your insurance company doesn't want to pay, who pays? If you want to get back in business you're probably going to have to pay out of your pocket and then later try to convince the landlord to pay or maybe the landlord will try to get their insurance company to pay. So just be ready for issues like that but you're sometimes going to have to pay out of pocket upfront to get your business going again and then later try to get reimbursed.

I have the same issue happen one time with one of my locations where some homeless guys were out catching dumpsters on fire and they start a fire in the back alley of one of our offices and they caused $6,000 in damages to the electrical panel and to the electrical boxes. We were out of power for a week. Our insurance company was not going to pay because it was on the outside. The landlord did not think they were liable for it but we had to pay out of our pocket, get it fixed but our insurance company let us know that since we paid for that electrical box it now is part of our policy. So if we are unfortunate enough to have someone come and catch our electrical box on fire again then we will be covered in the future. Insurance is never easy to deal with but that is something that you need to have. You need to be able to protect yourself in case of fire or robbery.

By Year 5 your business probably has expanded and you probably have multiple employees now. Your company probably has maybe a general manager or a district manager that helps you run multiple locations. You probably have multiple employees, you probably have to deal with employees being hired and fired, lawsuits, labor issues, things like that.

The next few years of your company you are going to have plan out as far as do you expand further than the local city or county that you're in. Do you expand out of state? What is your age? When do you want to retire? How long do you want to keep growing until you get to a certain point that you are fine with the size and you want to just maintain that and maybe just grow each location instead of growing number of locations.

By Year 10 you probably have expanded even more and you'll want to look into other options to grow your company. You can look at an IPO, where you can become public. You can look at a stock options where you start letting your employees actually purchase stock and become part owners of the company. This has always been an incentive for employees to work harder. You may also be looking at selling your company to retire or semi-retire. We will cover that in the last chapter.

CHAPTER 24
TURNING YOUR BUSINESS OVER WHEN YOU RETIRE/SELLING YOUR COMPANY

Now the two things you have to consider when you start thinking of retirement is there anyone in your company whether they are related to you or not that is capable of running the business at the same or higher level. A lot of business people fall into the trap of automatically turning over the company to a family member because they want to keep the business in the family and that is great. Sometimes it works out but sometimes it does not just because someone is your son or your nephew doesn't mean that they're smart, doesn't mean that they're going to do a good job for the company.

It will be awful to put 20-30 years into the business, build it up turn it over to a family member and have them run into the ground to where it's worth nothing or even bankrupt specially if that was your retirement plan to get a generated income from your family business that is now bankrupt. Don't let emotion cloud your judgment.

Markus Aurelius was one of the great emperors of Rome and he was clouded and gave his empire to Commodus, who was one of the worst emperors in Rome's history. So make sure that if your sons or nephews that are going to take over the company that they start at the bottom, work their way up, learn the business, get a good education and know what they're doing.

So if you're going to retire and turn it over to someone either if you don't have someone in the company then why don't you start doing a job hunt and hire someone to take over as COO or as president of the company. If you get someone that is very good then you can semi-retire or retire and still have confidence that the company is going to keep doing well and you're going to be able to generate a retirement income from the company that you spent your life building.

So that is one option is to make sure that you have an heir apparent that is going to take over and you work really closely with them and actually let them take over your last few months so that you know that everything that you're in the middle of, and all the projects, short term and long term projects that you got going are going to continue once you step down.

If there is not anyone in the company and you can't find someone out of the company or you just don't want a percentage each month, you want a lump sum, you just want to get out of the business then selling is the other option.

In some cases your upper management or your employees if they have ESOP maybe the ones that want to purchase the company so that is one option to look at. With your attorney you can also hire a business broker and these are brokers that specialize in buying and selling companies. They will have buyers and the first thing they'll do is they will do a valuation of your business.

Now you're probably going to think your business is more than what they look at because you have an emotional tie to your business. So if you think your company is worth $10M and they tell you it's $6M that's a big difference. It may be just the case that they just looked at raw numbers and in your business those are the numbers. In some cases they may be off so maybe you could find a different business broker or try to sell it yourself.

Either way your business' worth is subjective in some ways. While your sales are what they are and in some companies evaluation is just a simple 3x book value or 2.5 x book or 1.5xbook. It's just cut and dry that's what the business is worth. In other business they look at your sales, they look at your expenses, they look at value of your inventory and they look also at the value of any property that you have as part of the assets and they also considered goodwill.

If you're a single site location with two years in business the goodwill that you booked up, goodwill is actually your reputation in the community. But if you are by far is the best plumber, the best shoe store in the city and you have a 30 year reputation that is going to be worth a lot more, it is an intrinsic value but it is still a value. All those together are what make the total package of what your business is worth.

Now most of the time when someone is wanting to buy a business like yours they are going to want two things. One they would want to know that you are not going to open the same type of business to compete against them in the same area. So they're probably going to have a non-compete clause. It's hard to get bank financing for a purchase like this for a small business. So most of the time you're going to have to as the owner find a financing package, so let's say you're selling your business for $1M well you could set up a 5 year buyout $200K each year until the $1M is paid and in the meantime you'll own a lessening % of the business every year as the next $200K installment is paid. Basically you go from Year 1, 80% owner thenYear 2 down to 60% until you get down to 0% ownership.

Most business owners are going to want to have at least weeks or months of involvement with the leading owner so that there's a smooth transition with employees, with customers, with vendors, with everyone. They're also going to want some kind of liability protection so that if there are any lawsuits or issues before the closing date that they will not be responsible for those. That anything that happen before the date of closing is your responsibility.

There are tax implications to a business sale, capital gains and others whether it is stock or finance or a seller's finance purchase. So besides your attorney being your advisor on this you also need to include your CPA so that you don't get yourself into tax issues and the state tax and capital gains and all the other inheritance taxes that could be involve in this.

CHAPTER 25
CONCLUSION

In conclusion I hope that you picked up some helpful information from this book and also hope that it directs you to some great companies, suppliers and websites that can give you more help as you start working or continue your new small business. Having a small business is a dream for many Americans, it is the backbone of our country, you have all of the respect from people that have been too afraid to take the leap of faith that you did when you started your own company. It is a lot safer to have your steady salary, and your 401K and your benefits working for someone else but you took the risk and even though it's going to be a lot of work, you hopefully, will reap the rewards of that.

The key to success is belief in yourself, having a great product or service, doing a good job at it, keeping your customers happy. Your job is to keep your employees happy and their job is to keep the customers happy. If everyone does that your company will be very successful. Hire the best people, make sure that they do their job to the best of their ability, keep your word. Under promise, over deliver and you'll beat the odds and not only will your company survive but you'll succeed. Good Luck!

www.ingramcontent.com/pod-product-compliance
Lightning Source LLC
Chambersburg PA
CBHW051530170526
45165CB00002B/676